Styx

A Bilingual Edition

Else Lasker-Schüler

Mildred Faintly
translator

Ben Yehuda Press
Teaneck, New Jersey

Published by Ben Yehuda Press
122 Ayers Court #1B
Teaneck, NJ 07666

http://www.BenYehudaPress.com

To subscribe to our monthly book club and support independent Jewish publishing, visit https://www.patreon.com/BenYehudaPress

Jewish Poetry Project #43   http://jpoetry.us

Ben Yehuda Press books may be purchased at a discount by synagogues, book clubs, and other institutions buying in bulk. For information, please email markets@BenYehudaPress.com

Cover illustration adopted from painting of Else Lasker-Schüler. by Stanislaus Stückgold.

ISBN13 978-1-963475-58-6 pb 978-1-963475-59-3 epub

Library of Congress Cataloging-in-Publication Data

24 25 26 27 / 10 9 8 7 6 5 4 3 2 1   240719

Introduction

Styx, Else Lasker-Schüler's first book, appeared in 1901, when she was thirty-four. It has never been translated into English, though a few poems from it have appeared in the very few English translations of her selected poems.

Lasker-Schüler was one of the few women at the center of the German Expressionist movement, and the only woman poet among them. Her first book, the lucid work of a mature author, written and considered for over a decade before its publication, contains the full range of her themes, exquisitely arranged.

Here I will offer a brief biographical sketch, focused on the earlier part of her life, insofar as it will enrich one's understanding of the poems in this book. Else Lasker-Schüler (1869-1945) was born on February 11th, to a middle-class German-Jewish family in Wuppertal, in the far west of mid-Germany—in North Rhine-Westphalia, a little east of Dusseldorf. She was the sixth of seven children. Her father was a small-scale banker and dealer in real estate: a puckish, genial, good-natured papa. Her mother was a housewife with a taste for poetry.

Else received what would today be considered a high school education at a girls' school. Her childhood was fairly idyllic, though low-key antisemitism, no worse than name-calling, was an occasional feature of her childhood landscape, coming to the fore when the economy was bad. Like her parents, who prided themselves on being modern educated Germans as well as Jews, Else grew up with a love for her corner of Germany, a love which extended to its regional accent and ballads. She also adopted her parents' cultural, rather than observant, attachment to Judaism.

Two decisive losses marked her childhood and youth, and they inspired some of her finest poems. First was the death of her eight years older brother, Paul, of tuberculosis, in 1882, when he was twenty-one and Else was thirteen. Paul was religiously inclined and in the process of converting to Catholicism. He was the kind of older brother who is a friend and a mentor to a younger sister, and Else adored him.

Else's mother died in 1890, when she was fifty and Else was twenty-one. Else was unusually close to her mother, and this second loss cast a faint but steady shadow over the rest of her life.

In 1894, at age twenty-five, she married the physician Berthold Lasker, whose younger brother, Emanuel, became a world chess champion. Berthold himself was an accomplished chess player, as well as an amateur author and philosopher.

Shortly after their marriage, they moved to Berlin, for the sake of Berthold's professional advancement. While her husband was founding his medical practice, Else busied herself with art lessons, which led her to discover Berlin's bohemia.

Though Else would become friends with a great many persons whose names are still celebrated, from Martin Buber to Franz Marc, the one who had the greatest influence on her was the now forgotten Peter Hille.

Born a Catholic in 1854 (which made him fifteen years older than Else) in Erwitzen (in North Rhine-Westphalia, about a hundred miles to the east of Else's hometown), Hille dropped out of high school, and bummed around for the rest of his days. Actor, founder of a short-lived underground newspaper, novelist, hobo, ardent socialist—he promptly squandered the patrimony he inherited, and traveled through England, Italy, and Holland. He was a mystic, a turn-of-the-century German *saddhu* with the long hair and beard of a 1960's hippie. He claimed extensive knowledge of world religions, admired them all equally, and scorned the limits of scholarly scriptural knowledge. A childlike, ecstatic exponent of

Else Lasker-Schüler's Styx

free love, he let it be known that he could see into people's souls. He had an enthusiastic following among young people, and he became Else's guru.

Hille's novels, poems and epigrams survive, but they make for disappointing reading. He is a type frequently met with among bohemians: the charismatic man of the moment who seems to have his finger on the pulse of time, to transcend dreary norms, and think with true freedom.

But Hille's thought and insight should not be blithely underestimated. Lasker-Schüler's sometimes profound and always beautiful use of Hindu religious ideas is doubtless due to Hille. The Upanishads had been translated into German early in the 19th century and were greatly admired by Schelling and Schopenhauer, but Lasker-Schüler made use of the Upanishads' exalted concepts only so long as she was Hille's disciple.

Those who are familiar with the nineteen-sixties in America will have little difficulty picturing the alternative world of Berlin in the oughts. It was a haven of communes and social experiments, daring syntheses of science, art, and religion, inspired by counterculture heroes including Walt Whitman, Darwin, Nietzsche, and Giordano Bruno. This was the high tide of *Lebensreform* ("Reformation of Life"), a catch-all term for an amalgam of reform movements critical of materialism, industrialization, and urbanization, which idealized a return to nature. This was the intellectual milieu in which Else gained what served as her college education.

The older generation, particularly assimilating Jews like Else's parents, had seen the meaning of life in social advancement and material success. Their spirituality consisted in building splendid synagogues which they rarely attended.

Else found her spiritual home in The New Community (*Die Neue Gemeinschaft*), an artistic commune on the outskirts of Berlin, that lasted from 1900 to 1904, founded by Heinrich and Julius Hart, Jewish authors and journalists who advocated Naturalism (as opposed to Romanticism) in German literature. Another major player here was Gustave Landauer (also Jewish), a leading anarchist theorist. It should be evident that in turn-of-the-century Berlin, as in 1960's New York City, radical Jews were everywhere at the forefront of change and creativity.

The New Community was based in a former sanatorium with about thirty rooms, where some members lived paying minimal rent, and where Peter Hille lived free, in deference to his deliberate and spiritual poverty. Among the regulars were the future scholar of Hasidic mysticism Martin Buber and the occultist Rudolf Steiner. The painter Fidus, a minor *Jugendstil* luminary, painted the entrance hall with scenes inspired by Böcklin's *Isle of the Dead* to frame a centrally placed bust of Nietzsche. The events and gatherings here, or in rented halls in the city, ranged from neo-pagan rituals to poetry readings to concerts—usually combinations of all three. Else, who had a two-year-old by the time the commune opened, didn't become a full-time resident.

Else arrived in Berlin in 1895. Four years later, she had evolved from being a housewife and an art student, fresh from the provinces, into a woman of such advanced ideas that she had an illegitimate son, Paul, the afore-mentioned two-year-old. She proudly announced this child was not her husband's. Though she declined to identify the father, except as "a wandering Greek," it seems not implausible that Hille sired the child. Shortly before he died in 1904, Hille was at work on a novel to be called *Sappho* and dedicated to Else—which helps decode the phrase "a wandering Greek." The poem *Fallen Angel* (dedicated to 'Saint Peter Hille') in *Styx*, followed immediately by the poem *My Child* are, by my reading, a virtual birth certificate.

The marriage with Lasker of course could not survive this. Poems in *Styx* narrate the slow death of their embittered relationship so candidly and so frequently that they need not be enumerated here. A single anecdote will suffice to illuminate the pair's misery. Else had her child in a teaching hospital, under the eyes of medical students, because she could thus receive care without charge. Lasker wanted to cover the cost so that Else might be spared this indignity. Else said, "Of course his innate nobility triumphs over any sense of personal injury—that man makes me so sick."

Else's next romantic involvement was with Georg Levin. Born in 1878, this prize-winning Jewish conservatory student was a professional musician of twenty-two when he arrived in Berlin in 1900. A year later he'd changed his name to the more poetic sounding Herwarth Walden and become a vigorous participant in cabaret life. A cabaret was a combination of saloon, café, gallery, concert hall, and theater, which appeared in Paris in the 1880's and traveled east to Berlin around 1900. Most familiar to us in its later Weimar development, as a den of jazz music and decadence, its first form was far closer to a Beatnik coffee house. For Else, the cabaret was her natural habitat.

Her poems had appeared in a number of journals, and she had read from them at many gatherings public and private when her first book, *Styx*, was published in 1901 (though the year 1902 appeared on its copyright page). At this time Rilke and Hugo von Hoffmannsthal (Richard Strauss' librettist), were still young hopefuls, and the reigning German poet was Richard Dehmel, an author of socially conscious, Naturalist poems, whose more conventional effusions were set to music by the younger Schoenberg, Webern, and Weil. Else sent him her book and pestered him with letters, hoping he'd give her a leg up in literary circles—not realizing how entirely new her work was, or how impossible it would be for Dehmel to understand it.

By 1901 Walden was a Hille disciple and was setting Else's poems to music. They shared a passion for renovating art and society, and in 1903 she married him, narrowing the distance between his twenty-five years and her thirty-four by a tactful act of subtraction: she shaved a decade from her age. His parents were unenthusiastic about their boy's marriage to a clearly much older, divorced, unemployed poetess with a four-year-old illegitimate child. Nine years later, in 1912, the couple divorced.

Else's first book received some good reviews, the most prescient of which appeared in *East and West*, a journal founded by Martin Buber and Samuel Lublinski (a literary critic and historian of religion), to be the voice of the "Jewish Renaissance"—a renaissance which Buber would later understand to be possible only in Israel and in Hebrew. Lublinski wrote, "Whoever wants to know what's happening in modern poetry needs to read this book."

For this introduction to *Styx*, Lasker-Schüler's later career may be briefly outlined. Walden became editor of the Expressionist journal *The Storm*, and this placed Else at the very center of the Expressionist movement. She was close friends with the painter Franz Marc, who sent her hand-painted postcards. She evolved an outlandishly dressed social and stage persona that was a combination of orientalism and avant-garde theater. In 1932, she won the Kleist prize, the highest literary award of the Weimar Republic, previously conferred upon Bertolt Brecht and Robert Musil. Shortly thereafter, she fled to Switzerland to escape violent attacks from Brownshirts who targeted her as a celebrated Jewish author. She ended her days in poverty in Israel, supported by a loyal core of intellectuals in the German expat community.

Else-Lasker-Schüler was the only woman to play a leading role in the Expressionist movement. Her first book, *Styx*, is the first chapter in the history of Expressionist poetry. In her lifetime, her work caused considerable controversy. Rilke said, "She doesn't write, she barks." Kafka chimed in, "When the urban woman of today imagines she can think, the result is just such random cerebral spasms." To this day, her contribution is so little acknowledged that *The Penguin Book of German Verse* omits her entirely.

Rationale of the Translation

Comparing the German text with the translation, the reader may be surprised to see that the match is not precise. Frequently the translation is longer than the stanza it interprets, and even when the parallel poems proceed at the same pace, the rendering is not always word for word.

I have incorporated all the comments and clarifications one usually finds in footnotes into the text itself. The goal of a literary translation is to provide a coherent and complete experience of the text. This cannot be achieved where essential content is given elsewhere, and assembly is required. This applies not only to matters of history and natural history (like cloud formations or specific flowers), but the deep and multiple senses a poet can give to words when they are juxtaposed in startling ways. Imagine the result if we translated Dylan Thomas' *Altarwise by Owl-Light* word for word! Nothing would so betray the meaning of the poem as an overly faithful translation, which gave only one level of meaning where many coexist.

A Transgender Translation

Else Lasker-Schüler was somewhat rediscovered in Germany after the war, but she remains virtually unknown in the Anglophone world. There have been a handful of slender small-press renderings of her selected poems, which I fear will do little to improve her fortunes in English.

As a transgender woman, I hope to bring a new empathy to the translation of Else Lasker-Schüler. Male translators of poetry by women are not always intrigued by women's feelings. Typically, the images that best express them get flattened into abstractions.

Female translators of Lasker-Schüler rarely miss this dimension, but they dial down her strangeness. When Lasker-Schüler is made a poster-girl for women's literature, her image takes on the cleaned-up conventionality of a portrait on a coin or a postage stamp.

Thus has Lasker-Schüler been laundered: washed by women and pressed by men.

Else Lasker-Schüler described herself as "not so much a person as an atmospheric disturbance." She never fit in neatly anywhere. I don't believe her poetry can be fairly translated by anyone who did.

The Text

The German text follows that given in *Else Lasker-Schüler, Werke und Briefe*, Skrodzki & Oellers, Suhrkamp Velag 1996, which carefully reproduces the text and order of the first edition, brought out by Axel Juncker Verlag, Berlin, 1902 (actually 1901). The layout of the poems on the page, with their somewhat eccentric indentations, has been preserved. The spelling of German words has here and there been modernized where this does not affect the sound or the sense of the words.

I thank Julia Knobloch of Ben Yehuda Press for her excellent and sensitive reading of the manuscript. A real poet and an exceedingly well-read native speaker of German, she refined, enhanced, and bettered my renderings, and always did so graciously. Any remaining errors are mine alone.

Contents

Styx

Chronica

(Meinen Schwestern zu eigen)

Mutter und Vater sind im Himmel
Und sprühen ihre Kraft
An singenden Fernen vorbei,
An spielenden Sternen vorbei
   Auf mich nieder.
Himmel bebender Leidenschaft
   Prangen auf,
O, meine ganze Sehnsucht reisst sich auf
Durch goldenes Sonnenblut zu gleiten!
Fühle Mutter und Vater wiederkeimen
Auf meinen ahnungsbangen Mutterweiten.
   Drei Seelen breiten
Aus stillen Morgenträumen
Zum Gottland ihre Wehmut aus.
Denn drei sind wir Schwestern,
Und die vor mir träumten schon in Sphinxgestalten
   Zu Pharaozeiten.
Mich formte noch im tiefsten Weltenschoss
   Die schwerste Künstlerhand.
Und wisset, wer meine Brüder sind!
Sie waren die drei Könige, die gen Osten zogen
Dem weissen Sterne nach durch brennenden Wüstenwind.
Aber acht Schicksale wucherten aus unserem Blut
Und lauern hinter unseren Himmeln:
Vier plagen uns im Abendrot,
Vier verdunkeln uns die Morgenglut,
Sie brachten über uns Hungersnot
Und Herzensnot und Tod!
Und es steht:
Über unserem letzten Grab ihr Fortleben noch,
Den Fluch über alle Welten zu weben,
Sich ihres Bösen zu freuen.
Aber die Winde werden einst ihren Staub scheuen.
   Satanas miserere eorum!!

The Book of Chronicles
a poem written especially for my two older sisters

Our mother and father are in heaven
and their power jets forth
farther than echoes sing into the distance,
farther than stars sparkle with mischief,
all the way down to me.

The heavens tremble with the splendor of passion
as summer air shimmers with heat.
How it breaks forth, my longing to glide
along the rivers of light that pour from the sky
and are the sun's warm blood!

I feel my own mother and father sprouting
in the sky-wide womb of my expectant dread.
I feel three souls reaching out,
as far as nostalgia, a distance long as longing,
through morning's quiet dream
towards their Promised Land.

Those souls are we three sisters;
I remember how, before my present existence,
in the time of the Pharaohs,
we, in the form of sphinxes,
we dreamed.

I even remember how the Supreme Artist
first shaped me in the world's deep womb
with his heavy, monumental hand.

Know now who my brothers were!
—those very same three oriental kings
who followed their white star
through desert heat and sandstorm.

Eight were the dooms that grew like weeds
from my race, and still wait for us,
lurking beyond our heavens,

four to torture us at eventide,
four to darken our dawns;
they bring forth upon us the final and the direst:
hunger, being unloved, death!

Behold, it is written,
when the last of us shall lie in the grave
these things shall yet endure
to weave their evil spell over all the worlds
and rejoice in their own malice.

But the day will come when the very winds
will disdain to so much as stir their dust.
Then may Satan, their god, have mercy on *them*!!!

Mutter

Ein weisser Stern singt ein Totenlied
  In der Julinacht,
Wie Sterbegeläut in der Julinacht.
Und auf dem Dach die Wolkenhand,
Die streifende, feuchte Schattenhand
Sucht nach meiner Mutter.
Ich fühle mein nacktes Leben,
Es stösst sich ab vom Mutterland,
So nackt war nie mein Leben,
So in die Zeit gegeben,
Als ob ich abgeblüht
Hinter des Tages Ende,
  Versunken
Zwischen weiten Nächten stände,
Von Einsamkeiten gefangen.
Ach Gott! Mein wildes Kindesweh!
... Meine Mutter ist heimgegangen.

Mother

In July night a white star sings me a dirge,
in July night it rings out
a knell of light;
the humid darkness reaches down
its moist, exploring, shadowy hand,
trying to find my mother.

I feel how naked my body is,
I'm shoved off, like a boat from its dock,
leaving my motherland.

I never was this naked
since birth first bared me to Time,

I'm like a wilting flower left behind
when day's left, standing abandoned

to this wide night, and the next, and the next,
trapped in vast Alone.

O God, I cry like a child,
my mother went home without me.

Weltflucht

Ich will in das Grenzenlose
   Zu mir zurück,
Schon blüht die Herbstzeitlose
   Meiner Seele,
Vielleicht – ist's schon zu spät zurück!
O, ich sterbe unter Euch!
Da Ihr mich erstickt mit Euch.
Fäden möchte ich um mich ziehn –
Wirrwarr endend!
   Beirrend,
Euch verwirrend,
   Um zu entfliehn
      Meinwärts!

Out of This World

I want to return
to my original limitless existence,
to recover my own infinite,
to get back my Self, to get back to myself,

but already my soul's autumn crocuses,
those classic predictors of winter,
have flowered. Is it too late to return?

You're killing me, flowers,
stifling me with your petaled selves.

I wish I could just gather back my thread,
weave myself into coherence,
to baffle *you*, entangle *you*,
and escape back to myself.

Eifersucht

Denk' mal, wir beide
Zwischen feurigem Zigeunervolk
  Auf der Haide!
Ich zu Deinen Füßen liegend,
Du die Fiedel spielend,
  Meine Seele einwiegend,
Und der brennende Steppenwind
  Saust um uns!

. . . Aber die Mariennacht verschmerz' ich nicht!
  Die Mariennacht –
Da ich Dich sah
  Mit der Einen . . .
Wie duftendes Schneien
  Fielen die Blüten von den Bäumen.
Die Mariennacht verschmerz' ich nicht,
Die blonde Blume in Deinen Armen nicht!

Jealousy

Picture this: the two of us
camped out in a meadow
with those passionate people, the gypsies;
I lie on the ground at your feet
lulled to the soul by the music of your fiddle
while the wind moans over the plain—

I haven't gotten over that May Eve,
when I saw you with someone,
when wind ripped white petals from the dogwood tree
to fall like fragrant snow.
I haven't gotten over seeing that girl
fall into your arms like a blonde flower.

Frühling

Wir wollen wie der Mondenschein
Die stille Frühlingsnacht durchwachen,
Wir wollen wie zwei Kinder sein,
Du hüllst mich in Dein Leben ein
Und lehrst mich so, wie Du, zu lachen.

Ich sehnte mich nach Mutterlieb'
Und Vaterwort und Frühlingsspielen,
Den Fluch, der mich durchs Leben trieb,
Begann ich, da er bei mir blieb,
Wie einen treuen Feind zu lieben.

Nun blühn die Bäume seidenfein
Und Liebe duftet von den Zweigen.
Du musst mir Mutter und Vater sein
Und Frühlingsspiel und Schätzelein!
– Und ganz mein Eigen . . .

Springtime

We want to keep watch, like the moonlight,
all through the night, the quiet spring night;
we want to be like a pair of children.
You wrap me in your life,
you teach me to laugh
as only you know how to.

I grieved for the lack of a mother's love,
of a father's advice, of a springtime's play;
I grieved for the hard lot that drives me through life,
which I even began to grudgingly love
as one does a loyal enemy.

The trees wear flowers now,
delicate as silk, perfume falls from their branches,
sweet as love.
I need you to be my mother and father,
my treasure and my springtime's play,
mine only, mine.

Die schwarze Bhowanéh
(Die Göttin der Nacht)
(Zigeunerlied)

Meine Lippen glühn
Und meine Arme breiten sich aus wie Flammen!
Du musst mit mir nach Granada ziehn
In die Sonne, aus der meine Gluten stammen ...
Meine Ader schmerzt
Von der Wildheit meiner Säfte,
Von dem Toben meiner Kräfte.

Granatäpfel prangen
Heiss, wie die Lippen der Nacht!
Rot, wie die Liebe der Nacht!
Wie der Brand meiner Wangen.

Auf dem dunklen Schein
Meiner Haut schillern Muscheln auf Schnüre gezogen,
Und Perlen von sonnenfarb'gem Bernstein
Durchglühn meine Zöpfe wie Feuerwogen.
Meine Seele bebt,
Wie eine Erde bebt und sich auftut
Dürstend nach Luft! Nach säuselnder Flut!

Heisse Winde stöhnen,
Wie der Odem der Sehnsucht,
Verheerend wie die Qual der Sehnsucht ...
Und über die Felsen Granadas dröhnen
Die Lockrufe der schwarzen Bhowanéh!

Black Bowanéh

a gypsy song for the goddess of night

My lips glow like coals,
my arms spread like fire—
take me back to my Granada,
to the sun of southern Spain
where first I learned to burn.
My own fierce blood is pain to my veins,
my blood is strong, like wine,
with madness and heat.

Is any red so warm as that of a pomegranate?
Is any warmth so red as that of a kiss in the night,
a night of love,
warm with the red heat of an unseen blush?

Against my dark gleaming skin
shimmers a necklace of shells,
my hair is braided with amber beads
like sun-colored pearls, like flickers of flame.

My soul quakes, as only earth can quake,
cracks open as dry earth cracks,
thirsty for cool wind
summoned by the whisper of a river.

Hot winds moan like the very breath of craving,
terrible as the pain of craving.
Across the cliffs of Granada booms
the mating call of black Bowanéh.

Meine Schamröte

Du! Sende mir nicht länger den Duft,
Den brennenden Balsam
Deiner süssen Gärten zur Nacht!
Auf meinen Wangen blutet die Scham
Und um mich zittert die Sommerluft.

Du . . . wehe Kühle auf meine Wangen
Aus duftlosen, wunschlosen
Gräsern zur Nacht.
Nur nicht länger den Hauch Deiner sehnenden Rosen,
    Er quält meine Scham.

Shame Red

You! Stop wafting at me
the incense fragrance of your aromatic resins,
deluding daylight
with the sweetness of gardens at night
so the air shimmers as if with heat
and my cheeks flush blood-hot with shame.

Cool my face with a night breeze
blown over dewy lawns, aroma-free, wishless,
no more rosy exhalations of your yearning
that make my body
sweetly, shamefully ache.

Trieb

Es treiben mich brennende Lebensgewalten,
Gefühle, die ich nicht zügeln kann,
Und Gedanken, die sich zur Form gestalten,
Fallen mich wie Wölfe an!

Ich irre durch duftende Sonnentage ...
Und die Nacht erschüttert von meinem Schrei.
Meine Lust stöhnt wie eine Marterklage
Und reisst sich von ihrer Fessel frei.

Und schwebt auf zitternden, schimmernden Schwingen
Dem sonn'gen Tal in den jungen Schoss,
Und lässt sich von jedem Mai'nhauch bezwingen
Und gibt der Natur sich willenlos.

Drive

Hot, enormous, vital forces drive me,
feelings not to be bridled,
thoughts that take on shapes I nearly feel,
that fall upon me like wolves—

I stray, dazed, through fragrant summer days
and I make nights shudder with my high ecstatic cries.
My groans of pleasure are uninhibited
as those of a dying martyr—

afterwards, tremulous pleasure,
with shimmering wings,
floats over the sun-warm valley
of my young lap.
I'm defeated by a breath,
by May's least breeze,
Nature's willing victim

Syrinxliedchen

Die Palmenblätter schnellen wie Viperzungen
In die Kelche der roten Gladiolen,
Und die Mondsichel lacht
Wie ein Faunsaug' verstohlen.

Die Welt hält das Leben umschlungen
Im Strahl des Saturn
Und durch das Träumen der Nacht
Sprüht es purpurn.

Jüx! Wollen uns im Schilfrohr
Mit Binsen aneinander binden
Und mit der Morgenröte Frühlicht
Den Süden unserer Liebe ergründen!

Song of the Pan-Pipe

It was in a garden, possibly Eden,
a palm tickled the red depth
of a gladiolus' chalice with a green spear of leaf
that flickered like a serpent's tongue.
The silver reaping-hook of the moon
gleamed sneaky approval
like a faun's tilted grin.

This living world was clasped,
held fast in pale, cold Saturn's numbing rays—
who knew that night
would spurt purple dreams?

Hilarious, no? We two together,
tightened to each other like a pan-pipe's reeds.
Before dawn blushed
we'd fathom the southernmost
of love's deep notes.

Nervus Erotis

Dass uns nach all' der heissen Tagesglut
Nicht eine Nacht gehört ...
Die Tuberosen färben sich mit meinem Blut,
Aus ihren Kelchen lodert's brandrot!

Sag' mir, ob auch in Nächten Deine Seele schreit,
Wenn sie aus bangem Schlummer auffährt,
Wie wilde Vögel schreien durch die Nachtzeit.

Die ganze Welt scheint rot,
Als ob des Lebens weite Seele blutet.
Mein Herz stöhnt wie das Leid der Hungersnot,
Aus roten Geisteraugen stiert der Tod!

Sag' mir, ob auch in Nächten Deine Seele klagt,
Vom starken Tuberosenduft umflutet,
Und an dem Nerv des bunten Traumes nagt.

Till It Bleeds

Despite a day that glowed like a coal,
the dark hour's powerless,
no lulling in its lateness.
The night-blooming tuberose,
with sweet oppressive scent, prevents rest.
Its waxy white flowers, at stem's end, redden
to the color of my blood, the petals flame—
not flowers, but flares.

Do you too jolt awake from anxiety dreams
in the middle of the night, with a cry
like a wild bird's?

I see the whole world as through a red lens,
as if existence were a kind of hemorrhage;
my heart groans with a pain as real as hunger,
Death stares back at me with lamp-like eyes.

Does your soul grieve in the night like mine,
when the tuberose,
with all the perverse strength
in its swollen fleshy roots,
sweetly reeks, as if to drown you in flowers?
Does your soul gnaw and scratch
at your daytime life
till it bleeds?

Winternacht
(*Cellolied*)

Ich schlafe tief in starrer Winternacht,
Mir ist, ich lieg' in Grabesnacht,
Als ob ich spät um Mitternacht gestorben sei
Und schon ein Sternenleben tot sei.

Zu meinem Kinde zog mein Glück
Und alles Leiden in das Leid zurück,
Nur meine Sehnsucht sucht sich heim
Und zuckt wie zähes Leben
Und stirbt zurück
   In sich.

Ich schlafe tief in starrer Winternacht,
Mir ist, ich lieg' in Grabesnacht.

Winter Night
a composition for cello

Deeply I sleep in the winter night,
still as if stiff and this were the night
of the grave, as if at midnight
I'd simply gone out, and now
I floated forever in blackness
like a dead star.

All the happiness of life I leave to my child;
the abstract concept "Suffering,"
is all that remains of my pains.
The last trace of my longing for existence dies
with an involuntary twitch
of obstinate life,
unable even to remember what it wanted.

Deeply I sleep in the winter night . . .

Urfrühling

Sie trug eine Schlange als Gürtel
Und Paradiesäpfel auf dem Hut,
Und meine wilde Sehnsucht
Raste weiter in ihrem Blut.

Und das Ursonnenbangen,
Das Schwermüt'ge der Glut
Und die Blässe meiner Wangen
Standen auch ihr so gut.

Das war ein Spiel der Geschicke
Ein's ihrer Rätseldinge ...
Wir senkten zitternd die Blicke
In die Märchen unserer Ringe.

Ich vergass meines Blutes Eva
Über all' diesen Seelenklippen,
Und es brannte das Rot ihres Mundes,
Als hätte ich Knabenlippen.

Und das Abendröten glühte
Sich schlängelnd am Himmelssaume,
Und vom Erkenntnisbaume
Lächelte spottgut die Blüte.

The First of All Springtimes

The serpent hung from her hips like a belt,
its head stared up at me, a smug buckle.
Her hat had, as an accent,
not a bird-of-paradise feather
but an apple of paradise,
and all this loveliness made my blood race,
crazed with longing, same as hers.

There was terror in the way the primeval sun
revealed our primeval nakedness,
and its light, despite brightness,
had the melancholy splendor
of a dying fire. My face, like hers,
was pale with dread in those doleful golden beams—
the effect was quite becoming.

Who says fate isn't playful?
What could be more winsome
than this hour's puzzlement
when we trembled, lowered our bashful eyes
at this fairy-tale ending
that circled round like a wedding ring
to where it started, where we were one.

I forgot that she was my sister
I balanced on the edge of a spiritual precipice.
Her mouth was hungry and red as flame,
my lips quivered like a little boy's.

Evening gloried all around sky's rim
like a ruddy ouroboros.
Flowers on the tree of knowledge sparkled,
clearly enjoying the joke.

Mairosen
(Reigenlied für die großen Kinder)

Er hat seinen heiligen Schwestern versprochen,
Mich nicht zu verführen,
Zwischen Mairosen hätte er fast
  Sein Wort gebrochen,
Aber er machte drei Kreuze
Und ich glaubte heiss zu erfrieren.

Nun lieg' ich im düst'ren Nadelwald,
Und der Herbst saust kalte Nordostlieder
Über meine Lenzglieder.

Aber wenn es wieder warm wird,
Wünsch' ich den heiligen Schwestern beid'
  Hochzeit
Und wir – spielen dann unter den Mairosen ...

May Roses

He promised his two holy sisters
not to seduce me; amid May roses
he almost broke his promise,
but he remembered to make the sign of the cross,
and did so, three times.
The freeze was so intense
I thought I had been burned.

Now I lie in a gloomy pine forest
and autumn whistles a cold north-easterly poem
over my outstretched springtime limbs.

I wish that pious pair of caring sisters,
when next the weather's warm,
all the joys of holy matrimony—
so the two of us will go back to our game
among the May roses.

Dann

... Dann kam die Nacht mit Deinem Traum
Im stillen Sternebrennen.
Und der Tag zog lächelnd an mir vorbei,
Und die wilden Rosen atmeten kaum.

Nun sehn' ich mich nach Traumesmai,
Nach Deinem Liebeoffenbaren.
Möchte an Deinem Munde brennen
Eine Traumzeit von tausend Jahren.

Then

You came to me then, in the night, a dream,
in the calm star-fire-light;
my daytime life passed me, laughing;
the wild roses held their scented breath.

Now all I want is an April dream,
the revelation of your love,
to feel your lips hot on mine
and not to wake for a thousand years.

Abend

Es riss mein Lachen sich aus mir,
Mein Lachen mit den Kinderaugen,
Mein junges, springendes Lachen
Singt Tag der dunklen Nacht vor Deiner Tür.

Es kehrte aus mir ein, in Dir
Zur Lust Dein Trübstes zu entfachen –
Nun lächelt es wie Greisenlachen
  Und leidet Jugendnot.
Mein tolles, übermütiges Frühlingslachen
  Träumt von Tod.

Evening

My laughter came tearing out of me,
child-eyed, leaping in front of your door,
singing Day in the face of Night.

My laughter entered into you,
to blow the gloomy ashes from your coals,
to wake a joyful blaze,
but the echo came back shaky as an old man's cackle,
sulky as a teen,
my frisky springtime giggles quieted,
chastened, as if they'd seen
death in a dream.

Karma

Hab' in einer sternlodernden Nacht
Den Mann neben mir ums Leben gebracht.

Und als sein girrendes Blut gen Morgen rann,
Blickte mich düster sein Schicksal an.

Karma

Once, on a night afire with stars,
I killed the man lying beside me.

Towards morning, as his blood pooled,
and he breathed his last with a low coo
like a mourning dove,
I saw his dark fate was now also mine.

Orgie

Der Abend küsste geheimnisvoll
   Die knospenden Oleander.
Wir spielten und bauten Tempel Apoll
Und taumelten sehnsuchtsübervoll
   Ineinander.
Und der Nachthimmel goss seinen schwarzen Duft
In die schwellenden Wellen der brütenden Luft,
      Und Jahrhunderte sanken
      Und reckten sich
   Und reihten sich wieder golden empor
   Zu sternenverschmiedeten Ranken.
Wir spielten mit dem glücklichsten Glück,
Mit den Früchten des Paradiesmai,
Und im wilden Gold Deines wirren Haars
Sang meine tiefe Sehnsucht
    Geschrei,
Wie ein schwarzer Urwaldvogel.
Und junge Himmel fielen herab,
Unersehnbare, wildsüsse Düfte;
Wir rissen uns die Hüllen ab
    Und schrien!
Berauscht vom Most der Lüfte.
Ich knüpfte mich an Dein Leben an,
Bis dass es ganz in ihm zerrann,
Und immer wieder Gestalt nahm
Und immer wieder zerrann.
Und unsere Liebe jauchzte Gesang,
Zwei wilde Symphonien!

Orgy

Evening secretly kissed the budding laurel
which became, in our game, a temple of Apollo
when our over-strong longing tumbled us together.

Night sky poured darkness like perfume
into the slow-surging waves
of a wind rich in possibility
into which the centuries sank
and re-awoke, stretching themselves,
to stand, all golden, in the starry armor of destiny.

Our impossibly lucky gamble brought us
the fruits of May-month paradise.

From a place deep as wanting, my scream sang
over the halo of your tousled hair
like the cry of a primeval forest bird.

Your newly created skies fell,
invisible but evident as a wild sweet scent,
confounding my earth with a heaven
no one could have even known how to wish for.

We tore off whatever still covered us,
cried out, drunk from breathing in
the hard cider of such an atmosphere!

I bound myself so tightly to your life
that I faded into you,
recovered my shape, vanished again
into the untamed double symphony
of exultant, criminally innocent love
that didn't know right from song.

Fieber

Es weht von Deinen Gärten her der Duft,
Wie trockner Südwind über mein Gesicht.
O, diese heisse Not in meiner Nacht!
Ich trinke die verdorrte Feuerluft
   Meiner Brände.

Aus meinem schlummerlosen Auge flammt
Ein grelles, ruheloses Licht,
Wie Irrlichtflackern durch die Nacht.
Ich weiß, ich bin verdammt
Und fall' aus Himmelshöhen in Deine Hände.

Fever

The scent from your garden
blows over my face, like a dry south wind.
O heat and need of my nights!
I lean in to drink, like the smell of a bouquet,
the arid blast of my own burning.

Harsh, nervous light flickers
from my sleepless eyes,
I am my own will o' the wisp,
in me is the delusive-elusive flicker
which I follow into night,
well knowing I'm damned
to fall like a rebel angel
into your hands.

Dasein

Hatte wogendes Nachthaar,
Liegt lange schon wo begraben.
Hatte zwei Augen wie Bäche klar,
Bevor die Trübsal mein Gast war,
Hatte Hände muschelrotweiss,
Aber die Arbeit verzehrte ihr Weiss.
Und einmal kommt der Letzte,
Der senkt den unabänderlichen Blick
Nach meines Leibes Vergänglichkeit
Und wirft von mir alles Sterben.
Und es atmet meine Seele auf
Und trinkt das Ewige ...

Existence

Once I had a night-sea of dark wavy hair—
that's buried long since, God knows where.
My eyes were clear and bright as a brook—
that's one more thing that sorrow took.
My hands were pretty and pink as shells—
a lifetime's work sent that to hell.

Now comes the last one in this series,
after Time, Grief and Labor—Death.
He studies my form that ever alters
with an eye that never does,
and releases me even from dying
(which had already released me
from everything else).
What a relief!
My soul takes a deep breath of Eternity . . .

Sinnenrausch

Dein sünd'ger Mund ist meine Totengruft,
Betäubend ist sein süsser Atemduft,
Denn meine Tugenden entschliefen.
Ich trinke sinnberauscht aus seiner Quelle
Und sinke willenlos in ihre Tiefen,
Verklärten Blickes in die Hölle.

Mein heißer Leib erglüht in seinem Hauch,
Er zittert, wie ein junger Rosenstrauch,
Geküsst vom warmen Maienregen.
– Ich folge Dir ins wilde Land der Sünde
Und pflücke Feuerlilien auf den Wegen,
– Wenn ich die Heimat auch nicht wiederfinde ...

Love-Drunk

Your mouth opens for me like the grave—
this can't be good.
Your voice lulls, dulls my resolve.
I'm sinking, without the least resistance,
transfigured by some kind of death.

Your breathing makes my body glow like a coal,
I tremble like a rose in warm spring rain,
follow you into pleasant hell,
plucking, as I go, lilies made of flame.
And if I can't find the way back,
so what?

Sein Blut

Am liebsten pflückte er meines Glückes
   Letzte Rose im Maien
Und würfe sie in den Rinnstein.
   . . . Sein Blut plagt ihn.

Am liebsten lockte er meiner Seele
      Zitternden Sonnenstrahl
   In seine düst're Nächtequal.

Am liebsten griff er mein spielendes Herz
   Aus wiegendem Lenzhauch
Und hing es auf wo an einem Dornstrauch.
   . . . Sein Blut plagt ihn.

He's Got Problems

What he'd really like to do
is pluck the last May-month rose of my happiness
and throw it in the gutter.

He's got problems.

What he'd really like to do is trap
my soul's last tentative sunbeam
in his own black depression,

to snatch my playful heart
from its cradle rocked by spring breeze
and jam it into brambles.

He's got problems.

Viva!

Mein Wünschen sprudelt in der Sehnsucht meines Blutes
Wie wilder Wein, der zwischen Feuerblättern glüht.
Ich wollte, Du und ich, wir wären eine Kraft,
Wir wären eines Blutes
Und ein Erfüllen, eine Leidenschaft,
Ein heisses Weltenliebeslied!

Ich wollte, Du und ich, wir würden uns verzweigen,
Wenn sonnentoll der Sommertag nach Regen schreit
Und Wetterwolken bersten in der Luft!
Und alles Leben wäre unser Eigen;
Den Tod selbst rissen wir aus seiner Gruft
Und jubelten durch seine Schweigsamkeit!

Ich wollte, dass aus unserer Kluft sich Massen
Wie Felsen aufeinandertürmen und vermünden
In einen Gipfel, unerreichbar weit!
Dass wir das Herz des Himmels ganz erfassen
Und uns in jedem Hauche finden
Und überstrahlen alle Ewigkeit!

Ein Feiertag, an dem wir ineinanderrauschen,
Wir beide ineinanderstürzen werden,
Wie Quellen, die aus steiler Felshöh' sich ergiessen
In Wellen, die dem eignen Singen lauschen
Und plötzlich niederbrausen und zusammenfliessen
In unzertrennbar, wilden Wasserherden!

Viva!

This little wish runs hot through my veins
like a sparkle-mad wine from a fire-leafed vine:
I wish we were one strength, one pulse, one satisfying
passion, one love-song to the whole burning world!

I wish we were reaching skywards, like a pair of branches
when a sun-crazed summer day shrieks for rain
and a cloudburst answers,
I wish we'd live forever, so we could tear Death
from his grave and laugh because his supposedly terrible
silence is all he can offer in reply!

I'd like to see the ground rise
within our deepest canyon,
lift into cliffs, gush up summits
vast beyond reach,
I want us to lay hands on heaven's center,
to rediscover ourselves
with every breath, outshining all eternity!

I want a holiday just for rushing together,
we two, falling torrents
fountained down from precipitous cliffs,
thrilled by our own roaring water-song,
abruptly bubbling up, unendingly blending
into each another,
one flooding water-horde!

Eros

O, ich liebte ihn endlos!
Lag vor seinen Knien
Und klagte Eros
   Meine Sehnsucht.
O, ich liebte ihn fassungslos.
Wie eine Sommernacht
   Sank mein Kopf
Blutschwarz auf seinen Schoss
Und meine Arme umloderten ihn.
Nie schürte sich so mein Blut zu Bränden,
Gab mein Leben hin seinen Händen,
Und erhob mich aus schwerem Dämmerweh.
Und alle Sonnen sangen Feuerlieder
   Und meine Glieder
Glichen
   Irrgewordenen Lilien.

Love Itself

I loved him without limits.
Love itself knelt, clasped his knees and wept
for the depth of my longing.

I loved him till it dazed me
and my head sank in his lap,
my mind was dark as a summer night,
dark as blood.
My arms encircled him like fire,

I bound myself, like I never had to anything,
to his blaze. Into his hands
did I commend my spirit,
and he raised me from woe's twilight,
sunbeams sang the poem of fire,
I opened to him like a deranged lily.

Dein Sturmlied

Brause Dein Sturmlied Du!
Durch meine Liebe,
Durch mein brennendes All.
Verheerend, begehrend,
  Dröhnend wiedertönend
  Wie Donnerhall!

Brause Dein Sturmlied Du!
Und lösche meine Feuersbrunst,
Denn ich ersticke in Flammendunst.

Mann mit den ehernen Zeusaugen,
  Grolle Gewitter,
Entlade Wolken auf mich.
Und wie eine Hochsommererde
  Werde ich
  Aufsehnend
Die Ströme einsaugen.
Brause Dein Sturmlied Du!

Storm Song

All the fire of love within me
summons your thunder;
all of the water
my fire requires,
pour it and roar your storm-song
through my love,

appallingly, longingly,
threatening, echoing,
roar your storm-song,
quiet my wild-fire, I'm
choking on smoke—

O man with the look of a Jove cast in bronze,
grumble your thunder,
pour down from the clouds,
loose it like Zeus,
I'll drink your stream thirsty
as midsummer earth.
You! Roar your storm-song!

Das Lied des Gesalbten

Zebaoth spricht aus dem Abend:
Verschwenden sollst Du mit Liebe!
Denn ich will Dir Perlen meiner Krone schenken,
In goldträufelnden Honig Dein Blut verwandeln.
Und Deine Lippen mit den Düften süßer Mandeln tränken.

Verschwenden sollst Du mit Liebe!
Und mit schmelzendem Jubel meine Feste umgolden
Und die Schwermut, die über Jerusalem trübt,
Mit singenden Blütendolden umkeimen.

Ein prangender Garten wird Dein Herz sein,
Darin die Dichter träumen.
O, ein hängender Garten wird Dein Herz sein,
Aller Sonnen Aufgangheimat sein,
Und die Sterne kommen, ihren Flüsterschein
Deinen Nächten sagen.
Ja, tausend greifende Äste werden Deine Arme tragen,
Und meinem Paradiesheimweh wiegende Tröste sein!

Song of the Anointed

Thus saith the Lord at eventide:

Lovingly squander, and I will repay you
with the pearls of my own crown,
make your existence so sweet
your blood will turn to flowing gold, to honey,
I'll satisfy your palate with marzipan.

Be lovingly wasteful,
gild my festivals with molten joy,
make the gloom that shadows Jerusalem
bring forth clustering blossoms of song.

Your heart shall become a splendid garden
in which poets dream,
a city with terraces so densely set with trees
its seems more like a green mountain than a town;
even as Babylon among the seven wonders.

Your garden-city shall be
the rising sun's own homeland,
by night the stars will whisper it glimmering secrets,
and your arms will offer consolation like the shade
of a thousand upraised boughs, and thus shall you lull
God's own nostalgia for paradise.

Sulamit

O, ich lernte an Deinem süssen Munde
Zu viel der Seligkeiten kennen!
Schon fühl' ich die Lippen Gabriels
   Auf meinem Herzen brennen ...
Und die Nachtwolke trinkt
Meinen tiefen Zederntraum.
O, wie Dein Leben mir winkt!
   Und ich vergehe
Mit blühendem Herzeleid
Und verwehe im Weltraum,
   In Zeit,
   In Ewigkeit,
Und meine Seele verglüht in den Abendfarben
   Jerusalems.

Else Lasker-Schüler's Styx

A Song of Solomon

The sweetness of your mouth has taught me
only too well to recognize blessedness.
I already feel the lips of the archangel Gabriel
burn against my breast.

At night, clouds hover over my cedars
to drink their root-deep dreams.

Your life beckons to me
and I pass away into heartache
as the bud passes away into the flower—
I drift away skywards,
into time, into eternity,

my soul glows red
in the sunset over Jerusalem.

Kühle

In den weißen Gluten
Der hellen Rosen
Möchte ich verbluten.

Doch auf den Teichen
Warten die starren, seelenlosen Wasserrosen,
Um meiner Sehnsucht Kühle zu reichen.

Cool

I'd gladly bleed out
if I could thus share
in the white fire of a glowing rose—

but water lilies,
corpse-pale and still,
laid out on the pond,
cool my longing.

Chaos

Die Sterne fliehen schreckensbleich
Vom Himmel meiner Einsamkeit,
Und das schwarze Auge der Mitternacht
Starrt näher und näher.

Ich finde mich nicht wieder
In dieser Todverlassenheit!
Mir ist: ich lieg' von mir weltenweit
Zwischen grauer Nacht der Urangst ...

Ich wollte, ein Schmerzen rege sich
Und stürze mich grausam nieder
Und riss mich jäh an mich!
Und es lege eine Schöpferlust
Mich wieder in meine Heimat
    Unter der Mutterbrust.

Meine Mutterheimat ist seeleleer,
Es blühen dort keine Rosen
Im warmen Odem mehr. –
... Möcht einen Herzallerliebsten haben!
Und mich in seinem Fleisch vergraben.

State of Chaos

The stars flee from the emptiness of my sky,
as ever, white,
but now with terror.
The black pupil of Midnight's eye
widened to take me in.

Left for dead, no one will ever find me here.
I can't even find myself.
who I was is a world away,
my existence is now this state of dread
between two nights of non-being.

I even wish pain would return,
to shove me brutally down,
into sudden selfhood,
to yank me abruptly back into being me.

If only some creator's joy would beget me,
replace me in my native land,
under my mother's heart—

but that motherland is long since dead,
no roses bloom
fostered by her warmth.

If only I had a one true love,
I'd bury myself in his body.

Mein Blick

Ich soll Dich anseh'n,
 Immerzu.
Aber mein Blick irrt über alles Sehen weit,
Floh himmelweit, ferner als die Ewigkeit.
Du! locke ihn mit Deiner Sehnsucht Sonnenschein, –
Er wird mir selbst ein Hieroglyph geworden sein.

My Glance

I should always be looking at you,
but my gaze wanders beyond the visible,
it's flown beyond sky, past eternity.

Lure it back with a sunbeam of your desire;
without that, everything appears to me
cryptic as a hieroglyphic.

Lenzleid

Dass Du Lenz gefühlt hast
Unter meiner Winterhülle,
Dass Du den Lenz erkannt hast
  In meiner Todstille.
Nicht wahr, das ist Gram
Winter sein, eh' der Sommer kam,
Eh' der Lenz sich ausgejauchzt hat.

O, Du! schenk' mir Deinen gold'nen
Von Deines Blutes blühendem Rot.
Meine Seele friert vor Hunger,
Ist satt vom Reif.
O, Du! giesse Dein Lenzblut
  Durch meine Starre,
Durch meinen Scheintod.
  Sieh, ich harre
Schon Ewigkeiten auf Dich!

Miserable Spring

Since you felt the spring that was hidden by my winter,
since you recognized spring even in my dead silence—
it's miserable, being winter,
before summer comes, before spring restores joy.

Share with me your golden day,
a transfusion of your blood's red bloom—
hunger has frozen my soul like cold.

I'm weary of waiting so long ready-ripe—
give me a warm transfusion
of the springtime in your blood.

If I seem dead, winter-stiffened,
it's because I've been waiting for you
since eternity.

Verdammnis

Krallen reissen meine Glieder auf
Und Lippen nagen an meinem Traumschlaf.
Weh Deinem Schicksal und dem meinen,
Das sich im Zeichen böser Sterne traf.
Meine Sehnsucht schreit zu diesen Sternen auf
Und erstarrt im Morgenscheinen –
   Und ich weine
   Zu den Höllen.

Schenk' mir Deine Arme eine Nacht,
Die so frischen Odem strömen
Wie zwei nordische Meereswellen.
Dass, wenn ich aus Finsternis erwacht,
Mich nicht böse Geister treten,
Ich nicht einsam bin mit meinem Grämen.
Zu den Himmeln fleh' ich jede Nacht,
Doch der Satan hetzt die Teufel auf mein Beten.

Damnation

Claws tear at my limbs,
lips test my sleep, things nibble at my dreams.
Alas, that our two destinies met
under evil stars.
My longing howls at this,
even though, come morning, I'm just numb
and my tears fall into Hell.

Reach me your arms for a night,
they bring me fresh breath
as if they were North Sea waves.
Then no evil spirit will dare to stalk me
when I wake in the darkness
I want to be alone with my woe.
That's what I beg of Heaven every night,
but Satan sends devils to chase my prayers.

Weltschmerz

Ich, der brennende Wüstenwind,
Erkaltete und nahm Gestalt an.

Wo ist die Sonne, die mich auflösen kann,
Oder der Blitz, der mich zerschmettern kann!

Blick' nun: ein steinernes Sphinxhaupt,
Zürnend zu allen Himmeln auf.

Hab' an meine Glutkraft geglaubt.

The Ache of Existence

I, who was a burning desert wind,
cooled, took on a shape;

where is the sun that can dissolve me,
a thunderbolt to smash me?

See me now, a stone sphinx-head,
a fossil of rage against heaven—

I believed that my fire, that my fervor, was enough.

Mein Drama

Mit allen duftsüssen Scharlachblumen
Hat er mich gelockt,
Keine Nacht mehr hielt ich es im engen Zimmer aus,
Liebeskrumen stahl ich mir vor seinem Haus
Und sog mein Leben, ihn ersehnend, aus.
Es weint ein blasser Engel leis' in mir
Versteckt – ich glaube tief in meiner Seele,
  Er fürchtet sich vor mir.
Im wilden Wetter sah ich mein Gesicht!
Ich weiß nicht wo, vielleicht im dunklen Blitz,
Mein Auge stand wie Winternacht im Antlitz,
Nie sah ich grimmigeres Leid.
. . . Mit allen duftsüssen Scharlachblumen
  Hat er mich gelockt,
Es regt sich wieder weh in meiner Seele
Und leitet mich durch all' Erinnern weit.
Sei still, mein wilder Engel mein,
  Gott weine nicht
 Und schweige von dem Leid,
Mein Schmerzen soll sich nicht entladen,
Keinen Glauben hab' ich mehr an Weib und Mann,
Den Faden, der mich hielt mit allem Leben,
Hab' ich der Welt zurückgegeben
  Freiwillig!
Aus allen Sphinxgesteinen wird mein Leiden brennen,
Um alles Blühen lohen, wie ein dunkler Bann.
Ich sehne mich nach meiner blind verstoss'nen Einsamkeit,
Trostsuchend, wie mein Kind, sie zu umfassen,
Lernte meinen Leib, mein Herzblut und ihn hassen,
  Nie so das Evablut kennen
  Wie in Dir, Mann!

My Drama

He lured me
with every sweet scarlet flower.
I couldn't stand another night in that cramped room.
I went and stole myself some crumbs of love
right in front of his house—
while wanting him—
and that sucked the life out of me.
Hidden in me, a pallid angel weeps softly.
Soul-deep, I believe he fears me.

I saw my own face in the face of a storm,
I'm not sure how—in a lightning flash
or in the blackness just after.
My eyes, this much I know,
were two fierce-as-pain winter nights.

He lured me
with every sweet scarlet flower.
Something that hurts returns in my soul,
leads me far past any cause I can remember.
Be still, my wild angel,
let God keep his tears, his consoling words.
I won't unload my pain.

I've lost my belief in Woman, and in Man.
The ties that bound me to all that lives—
I return them to the world, unreluctant.

My suffering will burn like a sphinx in desert sun,
burn like a flower that sears the air with color,
burn like an evil spell.

What I long for now is the invisibility,
the solitude of a thing cast aside,
to hug my own loneliness for comfort, like a child.
I've learned to hate my body, and the life inside it,
and him. I've learned
that the real sin of Eve was loving a man.

Sterne des Fatums

Deine Augen harren vor meinem Leben
Wie Nächte, die sich nach Tagen sehnen,
Und der schwüle Traum liegt auf ihnen
   Unergründet.

Seltsame Sterne starren zur Erde,
Eisenfarb'ne mit Sehnsuchtsschweifen,
Mit brennenden Armen, die Liebe suchen
Und in die Kühle der Lüfte greifen.

Sterne in denen das Schicksal mündet.

Stars of Destiny

Your eyes wait for me
like a pain of nights that long for day;
in their depths, unfathomed, are uneasy dreams.

Your eyes, those strange stars, stare at the ground,
steely, while desires rove behind them,
like a pair of burning arms that snatch at love
and close on cold air.

Like stars that bring about a fate . . .

Sterne des Tartaros

Warum suchst Du mich in unseren Nächten
In Wolken des Hasses auf bösen Sternen!
Lass mich allein mit den Geistern fechten.

Sie schnellen vorbei auf Geyerschwingen
Aus längst vergess'nen Wildlandfernen.
Eiswinde durch Lenzessingen.

Und Du vergisst die Gärten der Sonne
Und blickst gebannt in die Todestrübe.
Ach, was irrst Du hinter meiner Not!

Stars of Hell

Why do you come looking for me,
in nights such as used to be ours,

through the clouds of my hate,
by the light of evil stars?

Leave me alone to fight with my demons.

They rush by on vultures' wings,
out of long-forgotten, distant wilderness,
like an icy wind blowing through the song of spring.

Now you forget your sunlit gardens,
you stare, cursed to share my grief.
What did you expect to find,
straying through my pain?

Du, Mein

(Meinem Bruder Paul zu eigen)

Der Du bist auf Erden gekommen,
  Mich zu erlösen
      Aus aller Pein,
  Aus meiner Furie Blut,
Du, der Du aus Sonnenschein
      Geboren bist,
Vom glücklichsten Wesen
    Der Gottheit
  Genommen bist,
Nimm mein Herz zu Dir
     Und küsse meine Seele
    Vom Leid
      Frei.

You, My Brother
for Paul, who died young

You came to earth to save me,
like the Christ you so admired;
to save me from every pain,
from my own rage.
You were born of a sunbeam,
God ransomed you back
into his own glad being.
Take my heart, brother,
kiss the sorrow from my soul.

Fortissimo

Du spieltest ein ungestümes Lied,
Ich fürchtete mich nach dem Namen zu fragen,
Ich wusste, er würde das alles sagen,
Was zwischen uns wie Lava glüht.

Da mischte sich die Natur hinein
In unsere stumme Herzensgeschichte,
Der Mondvater lachte mit Vollbackenschein,
Als machte er komische Liebesgedichte.

Wir lachten heimlich im Herzensgrund,
Doch unsere Augen standen in Tränen
Und die Farben des Teppichs spielten bunt
In Regenbogenfarbentönen.

Wir hatten beide dasselbe Gefühl,
Der Smyrnateppich wäre ein Rasen,
Und die Palmen über uns fächelten kühl,
Und unsere Sehnsucht begann zu rasen.

Und unsere Sehnsucht riss sich los
Und jagte uns mit Blutsturmwellen:
Wir sanken in das Smyrnamoos
Urwild und schrien wie Gazellen.

Fortissimo

You played a passionate song,
I was afraid to ask what it was called
because I knew its name would say everything
that had flowed between us
slowly as molten lava.

Nature co-authored this romantic pantomime
of unspoken heart's history.
The full moon laughed with her round fat face,
laughed light:
she was making us the heroes of a limerick.

Secret laughter shook our hearts' bedrock
even though our eyes seemed to float in tears
of deepest feeling.
The colors of the patterned rug
glowed a rainbow.

We both felt it—the Turkish rug
became a hallucinatory lawn,
palm trees swayed above us in the breeze,
our blood raced to keep up with these changes.

Our desires broke over us both in a wave,
brought us down as would a beast of prey,
we sank to the soft-as-moss carpet
with cries like those of two dying gazelles.

Der gefallene Engel
(St. Petrus Hille zu eigen)

Des Nazareners Lächeln strahlt aus Deinen Mienen,
Und meine Lippen öffnen sich mit Zagen,
Wie gift'ge Blüten, die dem Satan dienen
Und scheu den Lenzwind nach dem Himmel fragen.
Die heisse Sehnsucht hat mich tief gebräunt,
In kühler Not erstarrte meine Seele,
Ein Wetter stählte mein Gewissen!

Es wachsen Sträucher blütenlos auf meinen Wegen
Wie Schatten, die verbot'ne Taten werfen,
Und meine Träume tränkt ein blut'ger Regen
Und reizt mit seinem Schein zum Laster meine Nerven.
Die Unschuld hat an meinem Bett geweint,
Und rang und klagte dann um meine Seele
Und pflanzte Trauerrosen um mein Kissen.

Siehst Du den Kettenring an meinem Finger –
Sein Stein erblindete, sein blaues Scheinen,
Vielleicht verlor ihn mal ein Gottesjünger
Auf seinem Pfade hoch in Felsgesteinen.
Und diese roten, feurigen Granaten
Gab mir ein Königgreis für meine Nächte,
Wie heisse Tropfen auf die Schnur gereiht.

Fallen Angel
for Saint Peter Hille

Your face is more than haloed
by such a smile as Jesus, the man, must have had.
Looking at you, my lips part,
hesitantly, like the petals
of a poisonous flower, consecrated to Satan,
shyly asking the spring wind about heaven.
The fires of desire, real as sunlight,
have tanned my skin dark;
meanwhile, the cold of desperation
has solidified my soul, made it hard as ice,
my inner atmosphere has given me
a conscience insensitive as steel.

Plants that can't flower have grown, enclosing
my path, they lengthen
like the shadows of acts
of the kind that night invites. A blood-hot rain
drenches me in dreams, washing all things
into newness. Even sin seems clean.
Innocence lay in my bed and wept,
wrestled, then lamented, for my soul,
and finally departed, leaving on my pillow
a funeral wreath.

See this ring on my finger? A link of my chain.
Its gem, gleaming blue,
causes blindness. Maybe one of God's disciples
lost it on a steep path in the hills of Galilee.
These garnets, like coals you can hold?
A gray-bearded Herod gave me those in payment
for my young nights. Touch them!
Still warm from my neck,
this red necklace, warm as a string of tears.

Der Sonnenuntergang erzählt im Westen
Von späten Rosen, die ergrauen müssen
Im Herbste unter morschem Laub und Aesten,
Und nichts vom Sonnenglanz des Sommers wissen,
Als Sünderinnen sterben für die Thaten
Der eitelen Natur, die duften möchte
Noch in der späten Winterabendzeit.

Darf ich mit Dir auf weiten Höhen schreiten!
Hand in Hand, Du und ich, wie Kinder . . .
Wenn aus dem Abendhimmel wilde Sterne gleiten
Durchs tiefe Blauschwarz, wie verstoss'ne Sünder,
Und scheu in Gärten fallen, die voll Orchideen
Und stummen Blüten steh'n
In gold'nen Hüllen.

Und in den Kronen schlanker Märchenbäume
Harrt meine Unschuld unter Wolkenflor,
Und meine ersten, holden Kinderträume
Erwachen vor dem gold'nen Himmelsthor.
Und wenn wir einst ins Land des Schweigens gehen,
Der schönste Engel wird mein Heil erfleh'n
Um Deiner Liebe willen.

Sunset is telling the western sky
about how late roses have to fade
in autumn, when leaves are brittle
and branches are bare, and neither can remember
what a summer sun was—
like sluts they suffer in the end,
these late roses, according to the laws
they followed, the laws of amoral nature.
Now they offer their last perfume
as though that could warm a winter's night.

If only I could walk beside you through the heights
where sight becomes horizon wide;
if only we could go,
hand in hand, like a pair of children,
at an hour when untamed stars slip down the evening sky,
to fall from the blue-black, like sinners evicted
from heaven, to shyly land
in a garden full of night-blooming orchids
and day-flowers, enthroned in golden sepals,
with their petals closed like lips
that know how to keep a secret.

My innocence, a great flower-like cloud,
hovers just above the slender trees
that frame this fairytale,
and the sweetest dreams of my childhood waken
at heaven's golden doorway,
and when we pass at last into shut-eye country
the loveliest angel of all will implore
my salvation in the name of your love.

Mein Kind

Mein Kind schreit auf um die Mitternacht
Und ist so heiss aus dem Traum erwacht
Wie meine sehnende Jugend.

Gab' ihm so gern meines Blutes Mai,
Sprang' nur mein bebendes Herz entzwei.

– Der Tod schleicht im Hyänenfell
Am Himmelsstreif im Mondeshell.

Aber die Erde im Blütenkeusch
Singt Lenz im kreisenden Weltgeräusch.

Und wundersüss küsst der Maienwind
Als duftender Gottesbote mein Kind.

My Child

My child cries at midnight,
woken from a dream,
urgent as the fire
I felt in myself as a teen.

My mother-heart beats so panic-fast
it could just about split in two,
and would, to pour for my child's good
all the living springtime in my body.

A wintry moonbeam
adds a dire stripe to the night,
tigerlike, to a mother's fright.

But the earth, modest as a blossom
sings May's melody,
which the whole globe intones
in wind through the trees.

The sweet May breeze,
a scented angel,
gives my baby an invisible kiss.

Άθάνατοι

Du, ich liebe Dich grenzenlos!
Über alles Lieben, über alles Hassen!
Möchte Dich wie einen Edelstein
In die Strahlen meiner Seele fassen.
Leg' Deine Träume in meinen Schoss,
Ich liess ihn mit goldenen Mauern umschliessen
Und ihn mit süssem griechischem Wein
Und mit dem Öl der Rosen begiessen.

O, ich flog nach Dir wie ein Vogel aus,
In Wüstenstürmen, in Meereswinden,
In meiner Tage Sonnenrot,
In meiner Nächte Stern Dich zu finden.
Du! breite die Kraft Deines Willens aus,
Dass wir über alle Herbste schweben,
Und Immergrün schlingen wir um den Tod
Und geben ihm Leben.

Immortality

I love you into infinity,
beyond anything so limited as love or hate,
I want to possess you as light possesses a gem,
to shelter your dreams in my lap—
I'll build a gold wall around your soul,
toast it in sweet Greek wine,
anoint it with attar of roses.

I'll fly to you like a bird—to find you
in a sandstorm, in an ocean squall,
in sunset's red,
among the stars of my night.
Send forth the power of your will,
we'll float above all autumn,
immortal, evergreen,
we'll embrace even death
and give him life.

Selbstmord

Wilde Fratzen schneidet der Mond in den Sumpf
  Und dumpf
  Kreist die Welt.
Hätt' ich nur die Welt überstanden!
Damals als wir uns beide fanden
Blickte auch die Natur so gemein,
Aber dann kam der Sonnenschein
Und sang sein Strahlenlied
  Bis über den Norden.

Nun nagt der Maulwurf an Deinem Gebein,
In der Truhe heult die rote Katze.
Ein Kater schlich, sie lustzumorden
Aus vollmondblutendem Abendschein.
Wie die Nacht voll grausamer Sehnsucht blüht!
Der Tod selbst fürchtet sich zu zwei'n
Und kriecht in seinen Erdenschrein,
Aber – ich pack' ihn mit meiner Tatze!

For a Suicide

Moonlight shows me evil grinning faces
glimmering in the swamp.
The dull, muggy world turns.
If I could have endured other people!
But back when we encountered one another
it seemed as though Nature itself
was giving me dirty looks.
The sun, I admit, did rise,
with its song of light
reaching even the cold dark north.

I know that now the mole
gnaws your buried bones.
The full moon bleeds light;
a red cat is locked in the house,
shut up, as in a narrow cabinet,
howling to a tomcat slinking 'round outside,
a feral sex-offender.

Cruel desires unfold themselves
like night-blooming flowers.
Not even death likes such company;
he sneaks off to hide in his burial box
but *my* paw is fast enough to catch him.

Morituri

Du hast ein dunkles Lied mit meinem Blut geschrieben.
Seitdem ist meine Seele jubellahm.
Du hast mich aus dem Rosenparadies vertrieben,
Ich musst sie lassen, Alle, die mich lieben.
Gleich einem Vagabund jagt mich der Gram.

Und in den Nächten, wenn die Rosen singen,
Dann brütet still der Tod – ich weiss nicht was –
Ich möchte Dir mein wehes Herze bringen,
Den bangen Zweifel und mein müh'sam Ringen
Und alles Kranke und den Hass!

We Who Are About To Die

You wrote a dark poem in my blood
and it crippled my soul so it can't feel joy.
You drove me out of rosy paradise,
I had to leave all who loved me—
grief chased me away, like a vagrant.

At night, when roses sing their scented song
and Death silently broods
(over what, I am not sure),
I wish I could bring you my heart's hurt,
my frightened hesitation,
how I wrestle with myself to exhaustion,
and all my sickness and all my hate.

Ballade
(Aus den sauerländischen Bergen)

Er hat sich.
In ein verteufeltes Weib vergafft,
In sing Schwester!

Wie ein lauerndes Katzentier
Kauerte sie vor seiner Tür
Und leckte am Geld seiner Schwielen.

Im Wirtshaus bei wildem Zechgelag
Sass er und sie und zechten am Tag
Mit rohen Gesellen.

Und aus dem roten, lodernden Saft
Stieg er ein Riese aus zwergenhaft
Verkümmerten Gesellen.

Und ihm war, als blicke er weltenweit,
Und sie schürte den Wahn seiner Trunkenheit
Und lachte!

Und eine Krone von Felsgestein,
Von golddurchädertem Felsgestein,
Wuchs ihm aus seinem Kopf.

Und die Säufer kreischten über den Spass.
»Gott verdamm' mich, ich bin der Satanas!«
Und der Wein sprühte Feuer der Hölle.

Und die Stürme sausten wie Weltuntergang,
Und die Bäume brannten am Bergeshang,
Es sang die Blutschande ...

Und sie holten ihn um die Dämmerzeit,
Und die Gassenkinder schrien vor Freud'
Und bewarfen ihn mit Unrat.

A Ballad from the Hills of Westphalia

He fell for a devil of a woman,
and she was a devil of a woman for him to fall for,
his own sister!

She was affectionate, you have to grant her that,
she'd wait for him by the door like a cat,
Now a cat will lick the coin-hard calluses
on a feller's feet,
'cause it thinks of him as family,
and family gets groomed—
maybe it happened kind of like that?

The pair of them sat in the tavern
enjoying a day-drunk
with some pretty coarse company.

He rose up, wine-fed fire in his blood,
like an ogre lording it over some dwarves.

Standing at his full unsteady height,
it seemed to him he could see for miles.
Her laughter fanned his intoxicated flames.

A craggy crown of gold-veined stone
grew high on his head.
The other drunks, delighted, squealed.

"God damn, if I ain't the devil himself,"
said he, and hellfire spat from his wine-glass.

Seitdem spukt es in dieser Nacht,
Und Geister erscheinen in dieser Nacht,
Und die frommen Leute beten. –

Sie schmückte mit Trauer ihren Leib,
Und der reiche Schankwirt nahm sie zum Weib,
Gelockt vom Sumpf ihrer Tränen.

– Und der mit der schweren Rotsucht im Blut
Wankt um die stöhnende Dämmerglut
Gespenstisch durch die Gassen,

Wie leidender Frevel,
Wie das frevelnde Leid,
Überaltert dem lässigen Leben.

Und er sieht die Weiber so eigen an,
Und sie fürchten sich vor dem stillen Mann
Mit dem Totenkopf.

A storm began roaring like the end of the world,
lightning kindled a hillside grove
and the wind howled out his secret:
Incest!

They dragged him outside in the twilight,
street-kids pelted him with garbage,
screaming with glee.

Every year now on this same night
ghosts show, pious people hide
at home and pray.

Mourning really became his sister,
the rich innkeeper married her;
her tearful eyes will o' the wisped
him into her swamp.

Every year on this haunted night,
the sinner who did it with his own kin,
staggers impalpably down twilight streets
in blood-red sunset.

His dreadful sin, his sudden end,
put any normal post-mortem existence
out of the question.

He gives women such peculiar looks,
this wordless man with a skull for a head,
it makes them quite uncomfortable.

Königswille

Ich will vom Leben der gazellenschlanken
Mädchen mit glühenden Rosengedanken,
Wenn glanzlose Sterne mein Sterbelied singen
Und bleiche Winde durch die Totenstadt weh'n
Und vom Licht mein warmes Leben erzwingen.

Ich will vom Leben der wettergebräunten
Knaben, die nie eine Träne weinten,
Wenn die Tode vor meinen Herztoren steh'n
Und mit der Kraft meiner Seele ringen.

Ich will vom Leben der weissen Gluten
Der Sonne und von der Wolke Morgenbluten
Dem quellenden Rot der Himmelsbrust.
Bis meine Lippen sich wieder färben
Und junger Odem durchströmt meine Brust ...
Ich will nicht sterben!

The King's Will

I wish I could live, as any maiden does,
a girl gazelle-slender,
whose thoughts are rose-petal tender—
I don't want to be dirged
under dull unsparkling stars
when death comes, like cool wind
through a gray city, to steal my light
while my body's still warm.

I wish I could live, like a suntanned boy
who's never really known what it means to cry,
never feel in my final heart-beats
death knocking at the door of my life.

I wish I could live, like the sun's white warmth,
like the red clouds that flower at dawn,
drinking new life from heaven's breast,
I wish just such a color
would come back to my lips,
that just such a breeze
would become new breath in my chest.
I don't want to die.

Volkslied

Verlacht mich auch neckisch der Wirbelwind
– Mein Kind, das ist ein Himmelskind
Mit Locken, wie Sonnenscheinen.

Ich sitze weinend unter dem Dach,
Bin in den Nächten fieberwach
Und nähe Hemdchen aus Leinen.

Meiner Mutter Wiegenfest ist heut,
Gestorben sind Vater und Mutter beid'
Und sahen nicht mehr den Kleinen.

Meine Mutter träumte einmal schwer,
Sie sah mich nicht an ohne Seufzer mehr
Und ohne heimliches Weinen. –

Folksong

Whirling winds tease and jeer.

"My child, the breeze
is the sky's wild child,
with sun-colored curls,
and it means no harm."

I sit here under my roof and weep,
I'm feverish, I cannot sleep,
so I mend a linen shirt.

Today is my mother's birthday.
Both my parents are dead.
They'll see their little boy
never again.

My mother once had a dreadful dream,
after that she never could look at me
without a sigh and a secret tear.

Dir

Drum wein' ich,
Dass bei Deinem Kuss
Ich so nichts empfinde
Und ins Leere versinken muss.
  Tausend Abgründe
Sind nicht so tief,
Wie diese grosse Leere.
Ich sinne im engsten Dunkel der Nacht,
  Wie ich Dir's ganz leise sage,
Doch ich habe nicht den Mut.
Ich wollte, es käme ein Südenwind,
Der Dir's herüber trage,
Damit es nicht gar voll Kälte kläng'
Und er Dir's warm in die Seele säng'
  Kaum merklich durch Dein Blut.

You

I weep because I feel in your kiss
such nothing. I feel myself sinking
deeper than a thousand abysms
into emptiness.

At night, when I feel most trapped,
I ponder how to tell you this gently—
I lack the courage.

I wish a south-wind could tell you,
a warm south-wind,
(so it wouldn't sound so cold),
to sing the understanding into your soul
so it flowed imperceptibly
into your blood, and you just knew.

Müde

All' die weissen Schlafe
  Meiner Ruh'
Stürzten über die dunklen Himmelssäume.
Nun deckt der Zweifel meine Sehnsucht zu
Und die Qual erdenkt meine Träume.

O, ich wollte, dass ich wunschlos schlief,
Wüsst' ich einen Strom, wie mein Leben so tief,
Flösse mit seinen Wassern.

Tired

Trying to sleep, I counted white sheep,
but I kept seeing them tumble
over heaven's edge.
Doubt muffles my longing
and suffering shapes my dreams.

All I want is wishless sleep.
If only I could find a river deep as life
in which to sink.

Schuld

Als wir uns gestern gegenübersassen,
Erschrak ich über Deine Blässe,
Über die Leidenslinie Deiner Wange.
Da kam's, dass meine Gedanken mich vergassen
Über der Leidenslinie Deiner Wange.

Es trafen unsere Blicke sich wie Sternenfragen,
Es war ein goldenes Hin- und Herverweben
Und Deine Augen glichen seid'nen Mädchenaugen.
Du öffnetest die Lippen, mir zu sagen . . .
Und meine Seele färbte sich in Matt,
Dumpf läutete noch einmal Brand mein Leben
Und schrumpfte dann zusammen wie ein Blatt.

Guilt

As we sat and talked
I noticed how pale you'd become. It scared me.
Staring at the lines pain etched in your face,
I kept on talking, not knowing what I said.

Our glances met.
It was like looking at the stars for answers,
it seemed for an instant as though once more
our fates were golden, interwoven.
Your eyes had the silken shimmer of a young girl's,
your lips parted to tell me something,
our shared life flared faintly

and I heard a dull and distant fire alarm
go off in my soul,
which then shriveled like a leaf.

Unglücklicher Hass
(*Versrelief*)

Du! Mein Böses liebt Dich
Und meine Seele steht
Furchtbarer über Dir,
Wie der drohendste Stern über Herculanum.

Wie eine Wildkatze springt
Mein Böses aus mir,
Und beisst nach Dir.
  Entrissen
Von Liebesküssen
Aber taumelst Du
In Armen bekränzter Hetären
Durch rosenduftender Sphären
  Rauschgesang.

Nachts schleichen Hyänen,
Wie brütende Finsternisse
Hungrig über meine Träume
Im Wutglüh'n meiner Tränen.

Unhappy Hate
a classical bas-relief in verse

I love you with all the evil in me.
My soul stands over you,
glaring down as balefully
as the most menacing star
that brought fate down on Pompeii.

The evil that's in me leaps out at you
like a wildcat, but bites only air.
You've sidestepped my love's teeth
along with my kisses,
to tumble into the arms
of hetairai, through rose-scented heavens
of drunken song.

Predatory night-thoughts,
predawn spawn,
slink like panthers
through the hungry jungle of my dreams,
in the hot tropics of my tears.

Nachweh

Weisst Du noch als ich krank lag,
  So Gott verlassen –
Da kamst Du,
  Es war am Herbsttag,
Der Wind wehte krank durch die Gassen.

Zwei kalte Totenaugen
Hätten mich nicht so gequält,
Wie Deine Saphiraugen,
Die beiden brennenden Märchen.

Painful Consequences

Do you still remember
how I lay so god-forsaken sick,
and you came—
it was an autumn day,
wind wheezed thought the narrow streets.

The cold eyes of a corpse
wouldn't have harrowed me
as much as your blue eyes
as full of magic fire
as sapphires, as fairy-tales.

Mein Tanzlied

Aus mir braust finst're Tanzmusik,
Meine Seele kracht in tausend Stücken!
Der Teufel holt sich mein Missgeschick
Um es ans brandige Herz zu drücken.

Die Rosen fliegen mir aus dem Haar
Und mein Leben saust nach allen Seiten,
So tanz' ich schon seit tausend Jahr,
Seit meiner ersten Ewigkeiten.

My Dancing Song

A dark dance tune booms through my soul,
shatters it, scatters the fragments;
the devil takes advantage of my mishap
to try and hug my soul to his own blazing heart.

Roses go flying out of my hair,
my life whizzes off in several directions;
I've danced like this for a thousand years,
ever since my first eternity.

Vergeltung

Hab' hinter Deinem trüben Grimm geschmachtet,
Und der Tod hat in meiner Seele genachtet
   Und frass meine Lenze.
Und da kam ein Augenblick,
Ein spielender, jauchzender Augenblick
Und tanzte mit mir ins Leben zurück
   Bis zur Grenze.
Aber das Netz meiner Augen zerriss
   Vom plötzlichen Lichtglanz.
Wie soll ich nun die Goldzeiten auffangen!
Meine Seele die Goldlüfte einsaugen!
Der Tod hat sich fest an mein Leben gehangen,
Ich fühle immer stilleres Vergessen ...
Himmelszeichen künden Unheil an im Westen,
In der Sackgasse brütet Frucht ein Nebelbaum
Und winkt mir heimlich mit den Schattenästen –
Ja! Meine Seele soll Beklemmnis von ihm essen!
Und ein Alb auf Dir liegen nachts im Traum.

Payback

Under your sad anger I languished,
death stayed overnight in my soul
ate up my springtime.
But there came an instant,
an exuberant gamesome instant,
that danced me back into life
to the farthest edge, the giddy brink.

Such sudden illumination
was more than my eyes could catch:
a gold-fish flash that rent my net!
I couldn't snag so many golden moments,
it was more gilding wind than I could inhale.

Death held onto me for dear life,
stilling me into oblivion,
baleful stars in the west foretold woe.
In a dead-end street, a foggy tree
was hatching apples,
beckoning to me with shadow-branches.
It wanted me to taste its paralyzing fruit,
and for a succubus to sit on your chest
while you dream, and choke you under its weight.

Hundstage

Ich will Deiner schweifenden Augen Ziel wissen
Und Deiner flatternden Lippen Begehr,
Denn so ertrag' ich das Leben nicht mehr,
Von der Tollwut der Zweifel zerbissen.

... Wie friedvoll die Malvenblüten starben
Unter süssen Himmeln der Lenznacht –
Ich war noch ein Kind, als sie starben.

Hab' so still in der Seele Gottes geruht –
Möcht' mich nun in rasendes Meer stürzen
Von schreiendem Herzblut!

Dog Days

I want to know what your eyes are roving after,
what it is you want so badly your lower lip trembles,
I can't take any more of this life
so bitten through by my own doubt-crazed rage.

How peacefully the mallow-flowers died
under the sweet skies of a spring night.
I was a child then, when they died,

and calm as they I let my soul rest in God—

but now I'm ready to fall upon you,
my blood's a hurricane screaming in my ears.

Melodie

Deine Augen legen sich in meine Augen
Und nie war mein Leben so in Banden,
Nie hat es so tief in Dir gestanden
Es so wehrlos tief.

Und unter Deinen schattigen Träumen
Trinkt mein Anemonenherz den Wind zur Nachtzeit,
Und ich wandle blühend durch die Gärten
Deiner stillen Einsamkeit.

Melody

Your gaze sinks into mine,
my life was never so bound as now
it is to thine.
My life never waded so deep,
was never so helplessly sunk
as now
in thou.

I wander in your shadowy dreams,
my wind-flower heart drinks night,
and blooms in the gardens of your calm solitude.

Elegie

Du warst mein Hyazinthentraum,
Bist heute noch mein süssestes Sehnen,
Aber mein Wünschen zittert durch Tränen
Und meine Hoffnung klagt vom Trauereschenbaum.

Tausend Wunschjahre lag ich vor Deinen Knien,
Meine Gedanken sprudelten wie junge Weine,
Ein Venussehnen lag vor Deinen Knieen!

Zwei Sommer hielten wir uns schwer umfangen,
Ich tauchte in den goldenen Strudel Deiner Schelmenlaunen,
Bis aus den späten Nächten unsere Sterbeglocken klangen.

Und Neide schlichen heimlich, ihre Geil zu rächen,
Die Wolken drohten wild wie schwarze Posaunen,
Wir träumten beide einen Schmerzenstraum:
Zwei böse Sterne fielen in derselben Nacht
Und wir erblindeten in ihrem Stechen.

Der erste Blick, der uns zu eins gehämmert,
Er quälte sich bis in die Morgenstunden,
Bis weh das Herz des Ostens aufgedämmert.

Elegy

You were my hyacinthine dream,
you're still my sweetest longing now,
but tears have blurred my wishes
and my hope now mourns beneath its ash-tree.

I sat at your knees for a thousand years
worth of wishes, my thoughts bubbling up
like new wine; I sat there and longed for you,
I was ruled by Venus.

We caught one another, held each other fast,
for two summers. I jumped feet-first
into the golden whirlpool
of your mischievous moods,
until one late night love's knell rang out.

Envy sneaked up to punish us
for its own hot wantings, menace-dark clouds
thundered their wild black trumpets
like blunderbusses.
We had the same nightmare: two fatal comets
fell from our shared night,
blinding us with stabs of light.

That first shared look, which forged us into unity,
turned out to be a hammer-hit
throbbing pain all night,
and dawn was a heartache rising in the east.

Da sprangen alle grausigen Sagen auf,
Träumte nur noch Plagen,
Alle Plagen erdrosselten mich
Und reissende Hasse kamen
Und verheerten
Die Haine unserer jung gestorbenen Liebe.
Und wehrten meiner Seele Flucht zu Gott,
Gramjahre bebte ich hin,
Krankte zurück,
Kein Himmel beugte sich zu meinem Harme!
Durch alle Sümpfe schleift' ich mein verhungert Glück,
Und warf mich müd dem Satan in die Arme.

I dreamed of strangling calamities
gruesome as a Norse saga,
red rending hate came, devastated
the died-young meadow of our love.
Hate cut off any Godward escape.
After grief-shaken years I still relapsed,
no heaven bent down to shelter grieving me.
I hid in swamps,
there my starved luck ground me down
till I was nothing but edge
and came at last to rest in Satan's arms.

Vagabunden

O, ich wollte in den Tag gehen,
Alle Sonnen, alle Glutspiele fassen,
Muss in trunk'ner Lenzluft untergeh'n
Tief in meinem Rätselblut.
Sehnte mich zu sehr nach dem Jubel!
Dass mein Leben verspiele mit dem Jubel.
Kaum noch fühlt' meine Seele den Goldsinn des Himmels,
Kaum noch sehen können meine Augen,
Wie müde Welle gleiten sie hin.
Und meine Sehnsucht taumelt wie eine sterbende Libelle.

  Giesse Brand in mein Leben!
  Ja, ich irre mit Dir,
Durch alle Gassen wollen wir streifen,
Wenn unsere Seelen wie hungernde Hunde knurren.
An allen Höllen unsere Lüste schleifen,
Und sünd'ge Launen alle Teufel fleh'n
Und Wahnsinn werden uns're Frevel sein,
Wie bunte, grelle Abendlichter surren;
Irrsinnige Gedanken werden diese Lichte sein!
Ach Gott! Mir bangt vor meiner schwarzen Stunde,
Ich grabe meinen Kopf selbst in die Erde ein!

Vagabonds

I wanted to go into day,
not miss a single sun, not a single gilded dust-mote,
to binge on springtime breeze
to my own sure undoing,
sunken drunk into the blood-deep mystery
of who I might be.
The trouble was, I wanted too much joy.
For that, I'd gamble life itself away.
My soul had barely begun to understand
the golden sense of sunlit heaven,
when the sight was washed from my dazzled eyes
by a wave of tears, and my longing tumbled earthwards
like a dying dragonfly.

Pour fire into my life,
I'll lose myself beside you.
We'll glide along like spirits
when our souls growl like hungry dogs
and hell whets our hot wants—
we'll beg all the devils to send us sinful whims.
Really, it's an outrage, how insane we'll be,
like a loud sunset, buzzing with colors,
brilliant beams of crackpot fancy.
O God, dark is the present unlit hour.
I fear such drear, rather than that black
I'd rather dig a hole
and bury my own head.

Herzkirschen waren meine Lippen beid'

Ach, ich irre wie die Todsünde
Über wilde Haiden und Abgründe,
Über weinende Blumen im Herbstwind,
Die dicht von Brennesseln umklammert sind.

Herzkirschen waren meine Lippen beid',
Sie sind nun bleich und schweigend wie das Leid.
Ich suchte ihn im Abend, in der Dämmerung früh,
Und trank mein Blut und meine Süssigkeit.

Der Schatten, der auf meiner Wange glüht,
Wie eine Trauerrose ist er aufgeblüht
Aus meiner Seele Sehnsuchtsmelodie.

Two Red Cherries

I wander like Cain, like the spirit of sin,
over moor, chasm, and crag,
past the last sad flowers waved by autumn wind,
unplucked in their fortress of bramble and thorn.

My lips were two red cherries once,
my sorrow has shut them and made them pale;
I searched for him, sunsets and into the night,
that's drained me of blood, of the sweetness of life.

There are shadows now in my sunken cheeks
where once love-blushes glowed,
like two dark flowers to lay on his grave,
and a funeral dirge is the song in my soul.

Die Beiden

Dem zuckte sein zackiges Augenbrau jäh
Wie der Blitzstrahl einer Winternacht,
Und jener mit dem süssen Weh,
Dem ringenden Eden im Auge,
Mit dem Himmelblond auf der Stirn ...

Ich senkte mich in Beide
Wie ein erleuchtendes Gestirn –
Und es war, als sei ich:
Ihnen ihr Blut zu verraten:

Er mit dem scharfen Stahl im Aug'
Träumte von Heldentaten
Im Dickicht meiner Urwaldaugen.
Und jenem, dem die Höhen des Parnassos
Mit Goldblicken winkten sternenwärts,
Ihm spannte ich zwei meiner wilden,
Ungezähmten Dürste ans Herz.

The Pair of Them

This one raised one eyebrow, sudden, tufted,
expressive as a lightning flash in snowy night;
the other—in his eyes Eden's delight
struggled with sweet melancholy
beneath his halo of blond hair.

Like a fateful constellation,
I let my influence sink into them both,
as if it were up to me
to hand them over to their own instinctual drives.

The first: his stare suddenly sharp
as the flash of a blade,
dreamed hero-deeds
when he saw primaeval jungle in my eyes.
The other: his golden glance was raised
to Parnassus and starwards
—to him I yoked
my untamed looks
and raced away with his chariot heart.

Meine Blutangst

Es war eine Ebbe in meinem Blut,
Es schrie wie brüllende Ozeane
Und mit meiner Seele wehte der Tod
Wie mit einer Siegesfahne.

Zehn Könige standen um mein Bett,
Zehn stolze, leuchtende Sterne,
Sie tränkten mit Himmelstau meine Qual,
Alle Abende meine Erbqual.

Jäh rissen sich ihre Willen los,
Wie schneidende Winterstürme.
Über die Herzen hinweg!
Über das Leben hinweg!
Und ihr rasender Mut wuchs Türme!
Und sie schlugen meine Blutangst tot,
Wie Himmelsbrand blühte das Morgenrot,
Und mein Blass schneite von ihren Wangen.

Deep Dread

There was in my blood a dreadful ebb,
like the drawback of waters before a tsunami;
I heard the oncoming ocean roar,
my soul fluttered
like a battle-flag's wind-shaken length
o'er the ranks of death.

Ten kings stood 'round my bed
like ten proud sunbright stars.
Like dawn, they drank in the dew of my pain;
like night, they watched over the woes of my race.

Suddenly, they made their move
with as bitter a will as a winter storm,
commanding the heart, commanding life;
their courage became my tower,
my dread fell dead,
dawn's torch flared
fear-pallor fell away
like snow from the face of their clear sky.

Im Anfang
(*Weltscherzo*)

Hing an einer goldenen Lenzwolke,
Als die Welt noch Kind war,
Und Gott noch junger Vater war.
Schaukelte, hei!
Auf dem Ätherei,
Und meine Wollhärchen fütterten ringelrei.
Neckte den wackelnden Mondgrosspapa,
Naschte Goldstaub der Sonnenmama,
In den Himmel sperrte ich Satan ein
Und Gott in die rauchende Hölle ein.
Die drohten mit ihrem grössten Finger
Und haben »klumbumm! klumbumm!« gemacht
Und es sausten die Peitschenwinde!
Doch Gott hat nachher zwei Donner gelacht
Mit dem Teufel über meine Todsünde.
Würde 10 000 Erdglück geben,
Noch einmal so gottgeboren zu leben,
So gottgeborgen, so offenbar.
Ja! Ja!
Als ich noch Gottes Schlingel war!

In the Beginning
a lively composition, to be played with the world as orchestra

I swung from a golden spring cloud
when the world was still young and God a new father.
I balanced myself on a big blue egg
(the sky's whole dome).
Sparks shot out of my wooly hair,
I sang ring around the rosie,
teased the full moon (my fat grandpa)
till he teetered; I nibbled mama sun's
gold cookie-crumbs, shut Satan up in heaven
—God I confined to smoky hell.
The pair of them wagged their fingers grandly
cleared indignant throats.
Winds whistled like a whip, I was in for a licking,
but then God thundered a couple of chuckles,
along with the devil, about my idea
of what constituted a deadly sin.
I'd give ten thousand earthly joys
to live again, so God-given,
so God-hidden, so out and out in the open!
Yes, like I did when I was still
God's brat.

Else Lasker-Schüler's Styx

About the Translator

Mildred Faintly holds a doctorate in Classics from Brown University, and taught Classics and History of Religions at Haifa University. She is a contributor to The Jewish Women's Archive, and reviews books for 96thofoctober.com.

The Jewish Poetry Project

jpoetry.us

Ben Yehuda Press

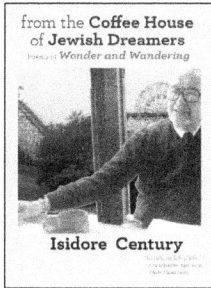

From the Coffee House of Jewish Dreamers: Poems of Wonder and Wandering and the Weekly Torah Portion by Isidore Century

"Isidore Century is a wonderful poet. His poems are funny, deeply observed, without pretension." – *The Jewish Week*

The House at the Center of the World: Poetic Midrash on Sacred Space by Abe Mezrich

"Direct and accessible, Mezrich's midrashic poems often tease profound meaning out of his chosen Torah texts. These poems remind us that our Creator is forgiving, that the spiritual and physical can inform one another, and that the supernatural can be carried into the everyday."
—Yehoshua November, author of *God's Optimism*

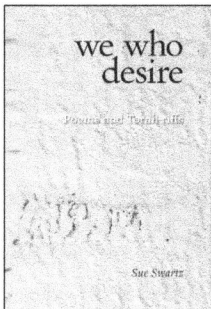

we who desire: Poems and Torah riffs by Sue Swartz

"Sue Swartz does magnificent acrobatics with the Torah. She takes the English that's become staid and boring, and adds something that's new and strange and exciting. These are poems that leave a taste in your mouth, and you walk away from them thinking, what did I just read? Oh, yeah. It's the Bible."
—Matthue Roth, author of *Yom Kippur A Go-Go*

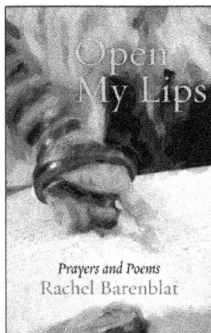

Open My Lips: Prayers and Poems
by Rachel Barenblat

"Barenblat's God is a personal God—one who lets her cry on His shoulder, and who rocks her like a colicky baby. These poems bridge the gap between the ineffable and the human. This collection will bring comfort to those with a religion of their own, as well as those seeking a relationship with some kind of higher power."
—Satya Robyn, author of *The Most Beautiful Thing*

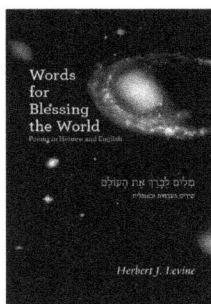

Words for Blessing the World: Poems in Hebrew and English by Herbert J. Levine

"These writings express a profoundly earth-based theology in a language that is clear and comprehensible. These are works to study and learn from."
—Rodger Kamenetz, author of *The Jew in the Lotus*

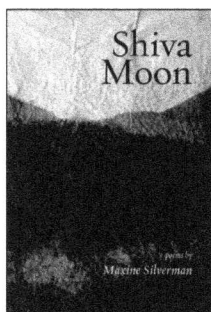

Shiva Moon: Poems by Maxine Silverman

"The poems, deeply felt, are spare, spoken in a quiet but compelling voice, as if we were listening in to her inner life. This book is a precious record of the transformation saying Kaddish can bring."
—Howard Schwartz, author of *The Library of Dreams*

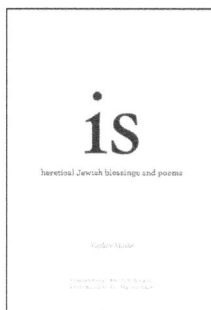

is: heretical Jewish blessings and poems by Yaakov Moshe (Jay Michaelson)

"Finally, Torah that speaks to and through the lives we are actually living: expanding the tent of holiness to embrace what has been cast out, elevating what has been kept down, advancing what has been held back, reveling in questions, revealing contradictions."
—Eden Pearlstein, aka eprhyme

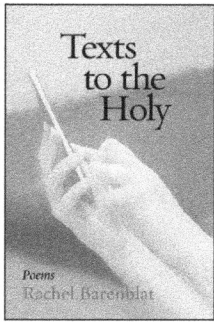

Texts to the Holy: Poems
by Rachel Barenblat

"These poems are remarkable, radiating a love of God that is full bodied, innocent, raw, pulsating, hot, drunk. I can hardly fathom their faith but am grateful for the vistas they open. I will sit with them, and invite you to do the same."
—Merle Feld, author of *A Spiritual Life*

The Sabbath Bee: Love Songs to Shabbat
by Wilhelmina Gottschalk

"Torah, say our sages, has seventy faces. As these prose poems reveal, so too does Shabbat. Here we meet Shabbat as familiar housemate, as the child whose presence transforms a family, as a spreading tree, as an annoying friend who insists on being celebrated, as a woman, as a man, as a bee, as the ocean."
—Rachel Barenblat, author of *The Velveteen Rabbi's Haggadah*

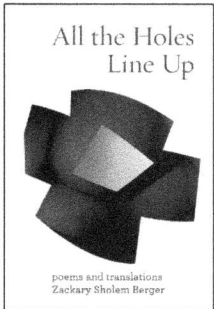

All the Holes Line Up: Poems and Translations
by Zackary Sholem Berger

"Spare and precise, Berger's poems gaze unflinchingly at—but also celebrate—human imperfection in its many forms. And what a delight that Berger also includes in this collection a handful of his resonant translations of some of the great Yiddish poets." —Yehoshua November, author of *God's Optimism* and *Two World Exist*

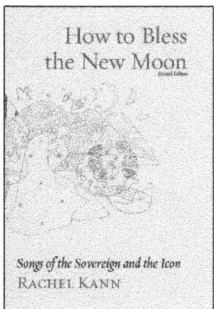

How to Bless the New Moon:
Songs of the Sovereign and the Icon
by Rachel Kann

"Rachel Kann is a master wordsmith. Her poems are rich in content, packed with life's wisdom and imbued with soul. May this collection of her work enable more of the world to enjoy her offerings."
—Sarah Yehudit Schneider, author of *You Are What You Hate* and *Kabbalistic Writings on the Nature of Masculine and Feminine*

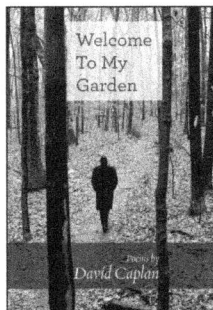

Into My Garden
by David Caplan

"The beauty of Caplan's book is that it is not polemical. It does not set out to win an argument or ask you whether you've put your tefillin on today. These gentle poems invite the reader into one person's profound, ambiguous religious experience."
— *The Jewish Review of Books*

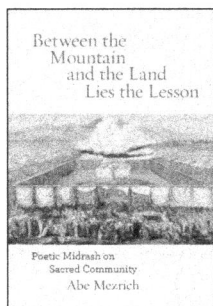

Between the Mountain and the Land is the Lesson: Poetic Midrash on Sacred Community
by Abe Mezrich

"Abe Mezrich cuts straight back to the roots of the Midrashic tradition, sermonizing as a poet, rather than idealogue. Best of all, Abe knows how to ask questions and avoid the obvious answers."
—Jake Marmer, author of *Jazz Talmud*

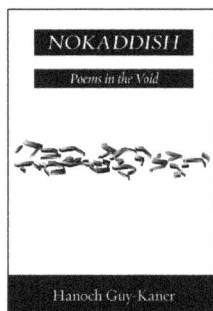

NOKADDISH: Poems in the Void
by Hanoch Guy Kaner

"A subversive, midrashic play with meanings–specifically Jewish meanings, and then the reversal and negation of these meanings."
—Robert G. Margolis

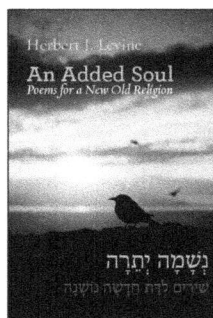

An Added Soul: Poems for a New Old Religion
by Herbert J. Levine

"These poems are remarkable, radiating a love of God that is full bodied, innocent, raw, pulsating, hot, drunk. I can hardly fathom their faith but am grateful for the vistas they open. I will sit with them, and invite you to do the same."
—Merle Feld, author of *A Spiritual Life*.

What Remains
by David Curzon

"Aphoristic, ekphrastic, and precise revelations animate WHAT REMAINS. In his stunning rewriting of Psalm 1 and other biblical passages, Curzon shows himself to be a fabricator, a collector, and an heir to the literature, arts, and wisdom traditions of the planet."
—Alicia Ostriker, author of *The Volcano and After*

The Shortest Skirt in Shul
by Sass Oron

"These poems exuberantly explore gender, Torah, the masks we wear, and the way our bodies (and the ways we wear them) at once threaten stable narratives, and offer the kind of liberation that saves our lives."
—Alicia Jo Rabins, author of *Divinity School*, composer of *Girls In Trouble*

Walking Triptychs
by Ilya Gutner

These are poems from when I walked about Shanghai and thought about the meaning of the Holocaust.

Book of Failed Salvation
by Julia Knobloch

"These beautiful poems express a tender longing for spiritual, physical, and emotional connection. They detail a life in movement—across distances, faith, love, and doubt."
—David Caplan, author of *Into My Garden*

Daily Blessings: Poems on Tractate Berakhot
by Hillel Broder

"Hillel Broder does not just write poetry about the Talmud; he also draws out the Talmud's poetry, finding lyricism amidst legality and re-setting the Talmud's rich images like precious gems in end-stopped lines of verse."
—Ilana Kurshan, author of *If All the Seas Were Ink*

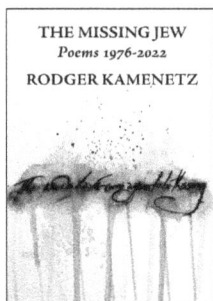

The Missing Jew: Poems 1976-2022
by Rodger Kamenetz

"How does Rodger Kamenetz manage to have so singular a voice and at the same time precisely encapsulate the world view of an entire generation (also mine) of text-hungry American Jews born in the middle of the twentieth century?"
—Jacqueline Osherow, author of *Ultimatum from Paradise* and *My Lookalike at the Krishna Temple: Poems*

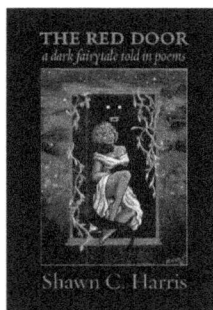

The Red Door: A dark fairy tale told in poems
by Shawn C. Harris

"THE RED DOOR, like its poet author Shawn C. Harris, transcends genres and identities. It is an exploration in crossing worlds. It brings together poetry and story telling, imagery and life events, spirit and body, the real and the fantastic, Jewish past and Jewish present, to spin one tale."
—Einat Wilf, author of *The War of Return*

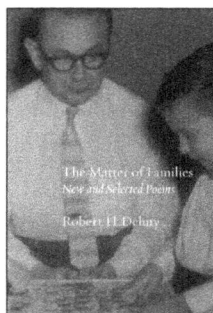

The Matter of Families
by Robert H. Deluty

"Robert Deluty's career-spanning collection of New and Selected poems captures the essence of his work: the power of love, joy, and connection, all tied together with the poet's glorious sense of humor. This book is Deluty's masterpiece."
—Richard M. Berlin, M.D., author of *Freud on My Couch*

The Five Books of Limericks
by Rhonda Rosenheck

"A biblical commentary that is truly unique. Each chapter of the Torah is distilled into its own limerick, leading the reader to reconsider the meaning of the original text, and opening avenues for interpretation that are both fun and insightful."
—Rabbi Hillel Norry

Bits and Pieces
by Edward Pomerantz

"A stunning tapestry of family life in the 40s and 50s. Like all great poetry, Pomerantz's work expands after reading. Each poem is exquisitely structured, often with a stunning ending, into a masterful whole."
—Alan Ziegler, editor of *SHORT: An International Anthology*

Words for a Dazzling Firmament: Poems/ Readings on Bereishit Through Shemot
by Abe Mezrich

"Mezrich is a cultivated craftsman— interpretively astute, sonically deliberate, and spiritually cunning."
—Zohar Atkins, author of *Nineveh*

Everything Thaws
by R. B. Lemberg

"Full of glacier-sharp truths, and moments revealed between words like bodies beneath melting permafrost. As it becomes increasingly plain how deeply our world is shaped by war and climate change and grief and anger, articulating that shape feels urgent and necessary and painful and healing."
—Ruthanna Emrys, author of *A Half-Built Garden*

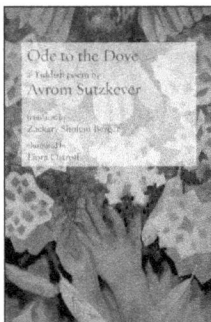

Ode to the Dove
An illustrated, bilingual edition of
a Yiddish poem by Abraham Sutzkever
Zackary Sholem Berger, translator
Liora Ostroff, Illustrator

"An elegant volume for lovers of poetry."
—Justin Cammy, translator of *Sutzkever, From the Vilna Ghetto to Nuremberg: Memoir and Testimony*

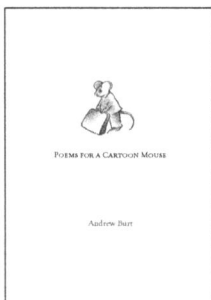

Poems for a Cartoon Mouse
by Andrew Burt

"Andrew Burt's poetry magnifies the vanishingly small line between danger and safety. This collection asks whether order is an illusion that veils chaos, or vice-versa, juxtaposing images from the Bible with animated films."
—Ari Shapiro, host of NPR's *All Things Considered*

Old Shul
by Pinny Bulman

"Nostalgia gives way to a tender theology, a softly chuckling illumination from within the heart of/as a beautiful, broken sanctuary, somehow both gritty and fragile, grimy and iridescent – not unlike faith itself."
—Jake Marmer, author of *Cosmic Diaspora*

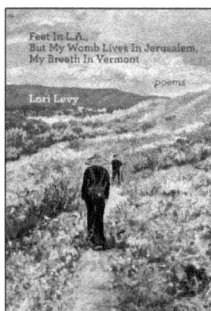

Feet In L.A., But My Womb Lives In Jerusalem, My Breath In Vermont
by Lori Levy

"Reading through Lori Levy's new book of poems takes my breath away. With no pretense whatsoever, they leap, alive, from the page until this reader felt as if she were living Levy's life. How does the author do it?"
—Mary Jo Balistreri, author of *Still*

www.ingramcontent.com/pod-product-compliance
Lightning Source LLC
Chambersburg PA
CBHW021404090426
42742CB00009B/1000